The Risk Takers:
The Story of
Two American Families

Leslie Simpson Hall

iUniverse, Inc.
New York   Bloomington

The Risk Takers:
The Story of Two American Families

iUniverse books may be ordered through booksellers or by contacting:

iUniverse
1663 Liberty Drive
Bloomington, IN 47403
www.iuniverse.com
1-800-Authors (1-800-288-4677)

ISBN: 978-1-4401-0760-3 (pbk)
ISBN: 978-1-4401-0761-0 (ebk)

Library of Congress Control Number: 2008941186

Printed in the United States of America
iUniverse rev. date: 10/31/2008

Leslie Simpson Hall

To my Family
Past, Present and Future

Contents

Preface

When I became interested in genealogy in the late 1990s I thought I knew everything I needed to know about my grandparents. I knew when and where they were born and when and where they died. I was excited and in a hurry to extend my genealogy research to past generations with a goal of going back as far as I could. When I hit the genealogical 'brick wall' on one of my family lines, the Comers, and could not trace them further back than the early 1800s, I stepped back and realized that there was more to genealogy than dates, places and number of children. I started thinking more about who my ancestors were, what their lives were like, and what decisions they had made that made a difference in their lives as well as in the lives of their children and grandchildren. I wanted to know more about how they lived their day-to-day lives and what challenges they faced.

Then July 3, 2003 arrived and I became a grandmother myself with the birth of Ryan Scott Cash. My interest in genealogy seemed to take on more importance and I wanted to capture as much information as I could to pass on to my children and my grandchildren including Ryan and Morgan Paige Cash (who arrived April 2, 2005), and future grandchildren who may bless my life. I decided that a book about my family would be the best way to insure that the information I had gathered would be passed on to my children and grandchildren in a meaningful way. I started with a journal-type book that I purchased with pre-designed questions to be answered. This was fun but limited my creativity and did not allow me to include all of the information I wanted to include. After attending a

Virginia Genealogical Society meeting in Richmond I was inspired by a genealogist and writer who described a method of writing about family history that utilized social history. Social history is the study of "ordinary people's everyday lives"[1] that adds depth, detail and drama to a family's story. Finally, I had the answer. I would write a book using this social history concept about my family. But how extensive would or should this book be? Should I try to go back as far as I had researched? Wow, that could prove a fairly daunting challenge! After considerable thought, I decided to limit this first writing effort to just my four grandparents, James and Jeanie Simpson and Orval and Jennie Crisler.

Then I got to thinking about their lives and the times in which they lived. Imagine the changes these four individuals experienced during their lifetimes. All were born in the 1890's long before many of the technological advances we take for granted today. No telephones, no radio, no television, no automobiles, let alone personal computers. Their homes were heated by wood stoves; they did not have the benefit of indoor plumbing. Yet, most of them saw these advances and many more during their lifetimes. They endured two World Wars as well as the Great Depression of the 1930s. They sent their sons off to war during World War II. They witnessed man's efforts to explore space and saw man walk on the moon in 1969.

But their lives were not very different from many other people born at the same time who lived through the same trials and tribulations of wars and depression. What set them apart in my mind was their willingness to be risk-takers. My Simpson grandparents were risk takers leaving their homeland and their families in Scotland to make a new life for themselves and their young son in the United States. My Crisler grandparents left the comfortable farm life of rural Indiana when my grandfather made a career change to become an accountant and moved himself and his family to the Chicago area, forever leaving the comfortable and familiar agrarian existence of rural Indiana behind.

I want you to know about these people who lived very ordinary lives. They were not royalty, they were not listed in the "Who's Who" directory and they were not politicians whose names appeared in the daily newspaper. Their families were, in fact, so ordinary that tracing them genealogically has been quite challenging at times. However, they were ordinary people who successfully managed their daily lives in exceptional ways. They were risk-takers in simple ways that made a great difference in their lives and the lives of their descendants. They were loving parents and grandparents who will be remembered by their grandchildren and hopefully with this book by their great grandchildren as well as their great-great grandchildren and generations to come.

Let me tell you more about them and how their risk taking has made all the difference for us.

"Nobody can do for little children what grandparents do. Grandparents sort of sprinkle stardust over the lives of little children."

Alex Haley

Acknowledgements

Thanks to:

My teacher—Dr. Darrell Hurst who years ago inspired me in his English Composition course at the local community college and helped me realize that I could write and gave me the confidence I needed to pursue this project.

My inspiration—In October, 2004 I attended a genealogy conference sponsored by the Virginia Genealogical Society in Richmond, Virginia where Sharon DeBartolo Carmack was a featured speaker. Sharon introduced me to the concept of writing a family history narrative. Her book *You Can Write Your Family History* was an invaluable reference for this first-time author.

My mother—Virginia Crisler Simpson for her patient assistance in answering a multitude of questions about my grandparents. I could not have accomplished this without her help.

My proofreaders—my sister, Lauran Simpson Weiss and good friend, Jeanne Pitsenberger—thanks to both of you for your help and encouragement.

And finally last (but certainly not least) my husband, Frank, who was always a willing sounding board. For his constructive criticism, consistent support and love.

Chapter 1
Orval Hamilton Crisler

Grandfather Crisler, Orval Hamilton, was born October 10, 1893[2] at his parent's home a few miles from the small, rural farm community of Mt. Ayr, Indiana to William Addison Crisler and his wife Minnie Delilah Hopkins Crisler. His middle name, Hamilton, came from his paternal grandfather, Hamilton Crisler. No one today knows where the first name, Orval, came from or why he was named that, but Orval never particularly liked his first name and as an adult often used just his initials, O.H. Crisler. Even in 1893 the boy's name Orval was not common and appears at the 398th position on the one thousand most popular list of boy's names for the 1890s.[3]

The Crislers trace their lineage back to the early 1700s from the Palatinate area of what is now modern day western Germany. Escaping the religious persecution of Protestants and the invasion of their homeland by the French monarch Louis XIV, the Crislers left Germany. They stayed for a short time in Rotterdam, Holland before sailing to America in a small sailing ship landing in Philadelphia about 1705. Initially they settled outside of Philadelphia (in Germantown), but after a few years moved to a more rural setting in Culpeper County (now Madison County), Virginia. There they joined a group of fellow German Lutheran countrymen known as the Germanna settlers.[4] Our Crisler ancestors accompanied their fellow church members from Hebron Lutheran Church on the Robinson River in Madison County, Virginia west to the Kentucky frontier through the Cumberland Gap in the early 1800s. After a short stay in Boone County, Kentucky our branch of the Crisler family moved to western Ohio and later to Indiana, initially to Bartholomew

1

County, then to Newton County where Orval was born. According to family tradition Matthais Crisler, the original German immigrant, had 'long preached to his children' to cross the mountains and find their fortunes. Up until Orval's generation, all of his ancestors were farmers.

Orval's mother, Minnie (named Clara at birth) Delilah Hopkins, traced her family back to New England and her ancestors probably settled in Connecticut during the early 1600s from England. Her ancestors moved from New England to Ohio, then to Illinois, where Minnie was born, moving westward with the hope of inexpensive, fertile land. Her family moved to Newton County, Indiana when she was a young girl. Minnie's parents, Jeduthan Simeon and Anice Rouse Hopkins, were farmers as well.

Anice and Jeduthan Hopkins, Minnie's parents circa 1865

The Crislers arrived in Newton County, Indiana from Bartholomew County, Indiana in 1861 when Orval's grandfather, Hamilton Crisler, purchased a 240 acre farm in Jackson Township several miles northwest of the not yet formed town of Mt. Ayr. [5] Hamilton and Mary Elizabeth were the parents of nine children, five boys and four girls, born between 1845 and 1865. Their eldest son, William Addison Crisler, was born in 1847 while the family lived in Bartholomew County. [6]

Hamilton Crisler Family circa 1895–Possibly Fiftieth Wedding Anniversary -- Hamilton and Mary Elizabeth Crisler surrounded by their nine children including William Addison, John Henry, Emily Jane, Sarah Alice, Archibald, James Alfred, Allison Wilson, Marjorie Ellen, and Margaret Lillian

Orval's father, William Addison Crisler, the second born and eldest son, lived at home as a young man in Newton County, Indiana until 1878 when he moved to Kansas and lived there for about two years. Like many other young men of that time he opted for a career in agriculture, although we know that for a short time he experimented with the grocery business in Mt. Ayr. Growing up on the farm he had learned the rudimentary skills of farming and had experienced invaluable on-the-job training with his father, Hamilton Crisler. Even though he was the eldest son with four brothers he probably could not expect enough land from his father to make a go of farming on his own in Newton County. By the latter part of the nineteenth century most land was becoming more expensive than it had been for their parents and grandparents who may have benefitted from the inexpensive land for sale as the states of the Northwest Territory became available for sale by the United States government. We don't know for certain why he moved to Kansas but with his skills as a farmer he could likely have moved west to work as a hired hand on a Kansas farm. Kansas was a young state having been admitted to the union in 1861 just before the outbreak of the Civil War and may have been attractive to an ambitious young man. We do know he returned home to Indiana after a two year absence and 32 year old William Addison was living with his parents in Newton County, Indiana when the 1880 census was enumerated. He apparently was working for his father since his occupation is listed as a farmer.[7]

William Addison met and married a local girl, Minnie (born Clara) Delilah Hopkins October 6, 1892.[8] He was 42 years old, she 34, considerably older than the norm for the 1890s when the median age of men marrying was 26 and for women 22 years. It is possible that they became acquainted when both were working in the town of Mt. Ayr, he as a grocer and she as a dressmaker and milliner (hat maker). Daughter Virginia remembers her father, Orval, telling her that his father, William Addison, worked in retail business in Mt. Ayr for a short time when he operated a grocery business prior to his marriage. We know little about their courtship or marriage and no known wedding photos are available.

William Addison Crisler--Orval's father

Minnie Delilah Hopkins—Orval's mother

William and Minnie's first born child, a son, Orval, was born a year later on October 10, 1893.[9] He was born at home on the family farm a few miles from Mt. Ayr. A physician was probably in attendance to assist 35 year old first time mother Minnie give birth. A photo of baby Orval was taken by a Rensselaer, Indiana photographer in early 1894 when Orval was about nine months of age.

Orval Hamilton Crisler age 9 months. Taken July 1894

Photography was still in its infancy in the early 1890s. Although the art of photography had been around since the 1840s, it's practice was limited to professional photographers like the famous Matthew Brady who captured still photos of soldiers and battlefield scenes during the American Civil War (1861-1865). Brady used the daguerreotype method, named after Frenchman Louis Daguerre. The daguerreotype produced photographic negatives on large silver plates. This method involved large, bulky equipment for the taking of the photo and a complicated developing process that could only be handled with ease by professionals. The individual sitting for his or her portrait was required to sit still for several minutes without moving or smiling while the photograph was taken. Nor did it allow for duplication of the photo. Each process produced only one photograph that could not be reproduced again. Despite these inconveniences Daguerreotypes stimulated a flourishing market in portraiture. For the first time in history people could obtain an exact likeness of themselves or their loved ones at an affordable cost, making portrait photographs extremely popular for those of modest means.[10] In the 1880s George Eastman, founder of the Kodak Company, invented flexible, paper-based photographic film and the first small box-type camera allowing photography to become accessible to the amateur as well as professional photographer.[11]

Mt. Ayr, Indiana, initially called Mount Airy, dates from 1882 when it was laid out by Lewis Marion, who set aside forty acres of his own 250-acre farmland for a town. Mr. Marion donated a plot for a school, a church, and a park. He stipulated that the park should be fenced. At the time baby Orval was born there was a hitching rack (or hitching post) around three sides of the park. The rack consisted of posts in the ground with a heavy chain link fence. Since horses and buggies were the mode of travel at the time, there was considerable need for the hitching racks. In 1890 Mt. Ayr was a thriving town of about two hundred citizens which increased with the arrival of the Chicago and Eastern Illinois railroad, linking Mt. Ayr and Newton County to Chicago, eastern Illinois, Evansville, Indiana and St. Louis, Missouri for passengers as well as freight and coal cars.

At its height of over three hundred individuals around 1900, Mt. Ayr consisted of numerous businesses that supported the thriving farming community. A grist mill ground flour and meal for human and animal consumption. A blacksmith shop repaired farm machinery and shod horses, an important and thriving business in a town which depended on horses as their only mode of travel before the turn of the twentieth century. A livery barn provided shelter and food for horses brought to town by their owners. Horses and buggies could also be rented from the livery barn. Across the street from the railroad depot was an inn to accommodate travelers. A full-time railroad station agent handled the freight business as well as the telegraph service for the community. A lumber and coal yard was built across the street from the railroad depot. Other businesses included a grocery store, a retail flour, meal and feed store, a dry goods store, a bank, a drugstore, a post office, a pool hall and a newspaper printing office. An ice business provided ice to homes for food storage prior to the arrival of electricity in the early 1920s.[12] Orval's mother, Minnie Hopkins, owned and operated a dressmaking and millinery business in her brother's (Carey Jeduthan Hopkins) merchandise store in Mt. Ayr until her marriage in 1892. Like other women at that time, once she was married she devoted herself entirely to housekeeping responsibilities and undoubtedly assisted her husband with a variety of farm chores.

In the latter part of the nineteenth century women were expected to wear a hat. To go outside without a hat was considered not just unfashionable, but rude—an incredible display of bad manners. And hats were not inexpensive, costing between twenty cents and seven dollars per hat which compares to spending between fifteen and six hundred dollars on a hat in 2008. The milliner was an invaluable member of the community, fashioning each hat by hand, unique to each owner. Minnie would have used straw, buckram, wire or felt as the basis for each hat. The best straw hat forms (Leghorn) were purchased from Italy, from the Leghorn district of Milan. So many hats and fancy goods came from Milan that the town name is the root of the word "millinery"–a purveyor of hats and fancy goods. To make a straw hat, Minnie would have started with a plaited (braided) straw hat form. After wetting the straw to shape, Minnie would have cut and set the hat, and then decorated it as much as the customer wanted or could afford. Millinery was one of the most popular professions for women in the latter part of the 1800s. It was an ideal opportunity for a woman to work for herself and make an excellent living. According to the 1870 census more than fifty percent of the women milliners were single. As was true for Minnie, many dressmakers and milliners rented space from a general store while some traveled house to house to serve their female customers.[13]

We know that the latter generations of Crislers were Methodists and they either attended church at the North Star Methodist Church several miles north of Mt. Ayr or the Mt. Ayr Methodist Church in the town of Mt. Ayr, just behind the school. The Methodists were the first denomination to establish a church in the area of Mt. Ayr, followed later by the United Brethren and the Baptists. Mt. Ayr Methodist Church was built in 1884[14] so it is likely that this is the church that Minnie and William, Orval's parents, attended. Orval's grandparents, Hamilton and Mary Elizabeth Blankenbaker Crisler, had arrived in Newton County in 1861. Since they are buried at the North Star Cemetery, it is logical to assume that they were members of that congregation. But when the church in Mt. Ayr was built in 1884, their children, including William Addison and his wife, Minnie probably moved their membership to the Mt. Ayr church. The North Star Methodist Church is no longer in existence. It burned down sometime after 1877 leaving the cemetery across the road from the church site. In addition to our relatives, Hamilton and Mary Elizabeth Crisler, there are numerous other relatives buried at the lovely, pastoral North Star Cemetery, including George William and Lottie Hazel Crisler, infants of William Addison and Minnie Crisler. A walk through that rural cemetery reveals gravestones of many Crislers and

Crisler cousins including Blankenbakers, Stuckers and Cooverts, all early settlers of Newton County, Indiana. The cemetery is still in use today and is well tended.

Although we do not know exactly what farm life was like for his parents when Orval was a young child, we can learn much from information available regarding Midwestern farm life in the 1890s. Most Midwest farmers in the years following the end of the Civil War raised hogs, milk cows, beef cattle, horses and less commonly sheep.[15] At the time young Orval was growing up horses had become more popular because of the proliferation of horse-drawn machines. Prior to that oxen or manpower were the primary methods for farm chores including plowing, cultivating and harvesting crops. Oxen cost half as much money and ate half as much food as horses, but horses were faster and their hooves could withstand the frosty ground during winter months. For all their hard work, the horses consumed thirty to forty pounds of hay and five to ten pounds of oats every day.

Most of what was produced on the Crisler farm in the 1890s was for home consumption. The corn crop provided food for the hogs, cattle, horses, and to a lesser degree, the family. Potatoes, hogs, cattle, chicken, eggs, and most garden crops were primarily for home consumption.

The farm year was a busy one year round for Orval's father, William. Oats were planted in April, corn in May. The rest of May and June were devoted to cultivating the new crops. Most farmers in the 1890s including William Crisler, used the sulky (riding) plow for cultivating their fields. William would have been seated on a small metal seat behind his team of two or three horses with the plow behind him. This type of plow was developed and patented in 1875 and was an almost instantaneous success because of its practical design.[16] His horses were large draft horses, probably weighing in at eighteen hundred pounds or more. They were truly the work horses of the farm and allowed farmers to be more productive than ever before. In addition to plowing and cultivating the fields, horses were used to haul manure to the fields and to bring in the hay crop.

Corn needed cultivation (weeding) between rows at least twice each spring. Hay was harvested in June or early July, oats and wheat in August and September. The early fall months were devoted to cleaning the barn and spreading manure followed by the corn harvest in late October, a very intense and busy period. Once the corn crop was in William would have gathered the corn shocks and hauled them to his barn or corn crib. At the same time he would have selected the best ears to use as seed for the next spring's planting. Known as open-pollinated corn, this method yielded about forty bushels of corn per acre, versus today's yield of 150 bushels and more per acre. Corn was fed primarily to livestock.

Wheat provided a source of direct income. Harvesting the wheat was another fairly intense process and farmers often worked collectively with their neighbors or family members to harvest their wheat crops.[17] Undoubtedly, William Crisler, got help from his father, Hamilton, and his younger brother, John Henry, and possibly even his brother-in-law, Ben Harris, when it was time to harvest the wheat crop. William would have taken his wheat to the local mill in Mt. Ayr for processing.

Orval's mother, born Clara Delilah[18], but nicknamed Minnie (probably because of her petite size) was a full-time homemaker following her marriage to William Addison. Like most farm wives of the time she had a very important role within the farm family. Most farm families of that time divided work responsibilities along traditional gender lines. Minnie would have managed the house and her children, while William was responsible for the barn, the animals, the fields, and the wood lot. In addition, Minnie most likely maintained the family's vegetable garden and the chicken coop while William cared for the orchard. Minnie may have also helped with the milking of the cows.

Imagine how difficult keeping house was for the housewife of the 1890s. No indoor plumbing, no electricity, and none of the modern conveniences for the kitchen that we appreciate today. Minnie probably made her own soap for household use, for laundry, bathing and general household cleaning purposes since commercial soap did not become available until 1900. Lye soap, a combination of lard (pig fat) and lye (made from wood ashes), was the most common type of homemade soap. The lard and lye mixture was stirred continuously over an outdoor fire for several hours until it was thick enough to pour into boxes where it would harden and be ready to use in about two weeks.[19]

She had no vacuum cleaner but depended on sweeping with a broom and taking her rugs outside to the back yard to be beaten with a wire rug beater. She had to pump her water for washing dishes, bathing and laundry from an outdoor well in the back yard. On laundry day, typically Mondays, Minnie would boil the dirty laundry to remove heavy soiling, and then scrub it with lye soap on a metal washboard. Once washed, the clothes would go to another tub for rinsing in cool water, then wrung out and hung on a clothesline to dry, summer and winter. Tuesday was usually designated as 'ironing day'. Minnie would have heated a flat iron weighing four to nine pounds on the wood stove in the kitchen. She then would have rubbed the heated iron over a piece of brown paper to remove the stove black, then over a piece of waxed paper to leave a slick residue. Clothes were then sprinkled with water to create steam and smooth the wrinkles. In addition to clothing apparel, she would have also ironed her table linens and curtains. Since clothing and household fabrics were made from natural fibers, mostly cotton, linen or wool, ironing was essential. She would have washed all of the oil filled lamp chimneys each morning after trimming or replacing the wicks. She would also have emptied any chamber pots that had been used during the night.

Once her garden started producing each summer, Minnie was responsible for canning the fruits and vegetables for the family's use over the winter months. The Mason jar used for home canning had been invented in 1857 by John Mason and was used by home canners in the 1890s when Orval was a young child. It consisted of a wide-mouth glass jar with a zinc lid.

Home canning was an important activity for the farm wife and Minnie would have taken great pride in the produce she had 'put up' by canning and preserving. A recipe for canning corn, probably from her mother-in-law, Mary Elizabeth Blankenbaker Crisler, and likely used by Minnie, was found in the Hamilton Crisler family bible written in pencil on the last page.

Canning Corn

> *"Dissolve 1 ¼ ounce of tartaric acid in 1 pint of water. Of this solution take one tablespoonful for every pint of corn after bringing corn to a boil. Also allow one teaspoonful of the solution to every pint of water. Put on the corn to make it boil. When you open for use, put 1 teaspoonful of soda to three pints of corn."*

A daily chore for Minnie would have been food preparation for her hard-working husband William and young son, Orval. Farm families usually had a large breakfast, a large noontime dinner and a small supper. Common meats for meals included ham, pork, and chicken. Stews and homemade noodles were also popular. Most farm wives utilized their own fruits and vegetables, either fresh or canned from the previous harvest. She would have cooked in her kitchen over a wood-burning cook stove and oven. Although bakeries were common in the cities, farm wives did their own 'scratch' baking. Cookies and biscuits made from their own wheat were baked daily. More complicated recipes like cakes, pies, and breads were reserved for a designated baking day when the entire day was set aside for baking.

Minnie would take the milk that William had milked from his cows each morning and evening to make butter, buttermilk and cottage cheese. She would have strained the fresh milk, put it into a separator and left it in a cool place, either in a root cellar or on a ledge in the well while she waited for the cream to rise to the top of the mixture. Once cooled, the fat would have been poured off leaving 'skimmed' milk. Minnie would then have poured the cream into a churn where it would have been agitated for several minutes until it turned into butter. Once the butter was made, she had no ice box or refrigerator to store it in. She would have stored it on the ledge in her well outside in her back yard, particularly if the weather was warm. The 'skimmed' milk would have been drunk or used to make cottage cheese. A gallon of skimmed milk made about one pound of cottage cheese. For cottage cheese the milk would have been heated to eighty degrees, salt and a rennet tablet would have been added to make the curds. Once the curds formed, the mixture would have been poured into a colander or through cheese cloth to drain off the whey (liquid portion). The whey would have been fed to the chickens, while the curds would have been cooled and ready to be eaten.[20] Orval would later tell his children that he enjoyed drinking the leftover whey. Cottage cheese would also have been stored on the well ledge during warm weather.

Another important chore for Minnie would have been caring for the chickens on the farm. Chickens were an important food source for their eggs and meat. The chickens would have to be fed and watered daily and their eggs collected twice daily. Eggs not needed by the family for their personal use would have been sold to neighbors or taken into town for sale at the Mt. Ayr grocery store. Minnie would have been responsible for butchering the chickens, gutting them, and plucking their feathers. All parts of the chicken were utilized, including the livers. Since there was no refrigeration, chickens had to be killed, plucked, gutted, and prepared for immediate use. This was often a Saturday chore in preparation for Sunday dinner.

As Orval grew he probably was given responsibilities or 'chores' of his own. Boys in the 1890s were characteristically required to cut firewood, pump water, clean stalls in the barn, feed livestock, help their mothers tend the vegetable garden, empty chamber pots and carry water, food, and messages to their fathers in the fields. He may have been as young as three or four years old when he was expected to feed the chickens or help weed the garden. [21]

Orval was three years old when a little sister, Lottie Hazel, was born to William and Minnie in December 1896. Lottie was only nine months old when she developed meningitis and died. Meningitis is a bacterial infection of the meninges, the covering of the brain and spinal column. It is most common in children between the ages of one month and two years. Today meningitis is only about ten percent fatal. However, in 1897, before the arrival of modern day antibiotics, there was no treatment available. Little Hazel, as she was called by the family, was laid to rest in North Star Cemetery not far from Mt. Ayr.

Funerals in the latter part of the nineteenth century were important events. Black mourning cloth was hung over all mirrors in the house of the deceased.

It was considered bad luck to look in a mirror because it was believed that the person would see the face of the next person to die. The clocks in the house were stopped at the hour when the person died and pictures were turned to face the wall. The family did not leave the house while the deceased person's body was still in the house and the body was usually kept in the parlor until the burial. It was customary to sit with the body during the mourning period, while the curtains were drawn and the shades pulled. A close family friend or relative was asked to host the ceremony and while the immediate family went to the cemetery, this host would remove all of the funeral drapes and return the house to its pre-funeral condition.[22]

Starting at age five, Orval attended the Mt. Ayr School, one of seven schools in the Jackson Township area of Newton County at the turn of the twentieth century. His first grade teacher was a first cousin, Flora Alice Parke, a daughter of his Aunt Marjorie Ellen Crisler Parke and her husband Nobel Kirk Parke. Flora was a sixteen year old girl when she began her teaching career and was probably between 21 to 22 years old when she taught Orval. The Mt. Ayr School, the largest of the Jackson Township schools, was located in the middle of the town of Mt. Ayr. It was a frame building consisting of two rooms downstairs, one for first, second and third grades, and one for fourth, fifth and sixth grades. Upstairs there were two rooms, one for seventh and eighth grades, and one for ninth, tenth, and eleventh grades. A bell tower graced the peak of the school building. Seniors (twelfth graders) always went to nearby Rensselaer for the final year of high school and graduation. [23]

Schools in rural Indiana in the late 1890s were typically publically supported. Farm families recognized the importance of publicly supported schools at an early date. The neighborhood schools in that area of northwestern Indiana usually served a four square mile area so that no child had to walk more than a mile to school. Local residents employed the teacher, typically a teenage girl in the spring and fall and a young man in the winter, when the older boys attended. Teacher pay was less than fifty dollars per month. A few teachers were high school graduates, most were not. An elementary education supplemented by attendance at one or more of the teacher institutes that the state normal colleges sponsored during the summer, was typical. But whatever their level of education, teachers had to be jacks of all trades—nurse, janitor, philosopher, peacemaker, wrangler, fire stoker, baseball player, professor and poet as well as teacher. The curriculum of the rural school emphasized reading, writing, arithmetic, and a smattering of history, geography and science.[24]

Orval, like other young boys his age around 1900 when they dressed up, wore short pants with knee or three-quarter length socks, sometimes white socks, in addition to long over-the-knee stockings. Older boys wore the new double-breasted jacket, matching knee length pants, shirt and tie.

Orval Hamilton Crisler age 12 years, circa 1905

Young boys usually wore a head covering, a sailor hat or a flat cap with peaks. [25]

When Orval was about eight years old his mother, Minnie, gave birth to a second son, George William Crisler. Sadly, George lived only eleven months. His death certificate indicates that he died from pernicious anemia. Pernicious anemia is a condition in which Vitamin B12 cannot be absorbed because the stomach doesn't produce intrinsic factor. Intrinsic factor combines with vitamin B12 and transports it to the bloodstream. Infants can develop pernicious anemia when the folic acid content of their formula is low. Before 1920 the disease was always fatal because there was no known treatment. It is difficult to say if this was really the cause of his death but certainly pernicious anemia in infants is rarely seen today. George William was buried next to his sister, Lottie Hazel, in North Star Cemetery outside of Mt. Ayr. Orval would have been almost nine years old when George William died. Orval's daughter, Virginia, remembers her father, Orval, showing her the gravestones of his little brother and sister in North Star Cemetery.

Orval continued his education at Mt. Ayr school through the tenth grade when his parents sold their farm in Newton County and moved about ten miles away to a larger, eighty acre farm three miles outside the town of Rensselaer.

Crisler farmhouse in Rensselaer, Indiana, circa 1920

Since Rensselaer is in neighboring Jasper County, Orval had to switch schools. As he entered the eleventh grade he made the move from Mt. Ayr School to Rensselaer High School. There he was one of 27 students, 10 boys and 17 girls, in the eleventh grade. One of his new classmates was Jennie Comer, a Rensselaer girl. Little did these two know at the time they were classmates that they would later marry and have a family together, but we will discuss that later.

The Crisler family had just settled in their new home in Jasper County, a few miles outside of Rensselaer when Orval's father, William, was bitten by a neighbor's dog. The dog was rabid and William soon became ill with rabies, or hydrophobia. Hydrophobia is a viral disease spread through the bite of an infected mammal. The rabies virus infects the central nervous system, causing inflammation of the nervous system tissues and ultimately death. A bite from a rabid animal in 1911 was always fatal and statistics reveal that an average of one hundred people each year lost their lives to rabies at that time. Today a rabies vaccine is very effective in preventing the development of the disease if a human is bitten. Early symptoms in humans who have not had the vaccine are non-specific, consisting of headache, fever, and general malaise. As the disease progresses, neurological symptoms appear and may include sleeplessness, anxiety, confusion, slight or partial paralysis, excitation, hallucinations, agitation, excess salivation, difficulty swallowing and hydrophobia (fear of water). Death usually occurs within days of the onset of symptoms. William certainly experienced many of these symptoms in the last few days of life as evidenced by one of the obituaries written following his death. The June 13, 1911 edition of the *Rensselaer Republican* wrote:

> *"William A. Crisler died at half past three o'clock this Tuesday morning after having remained since 3 o'clock Monday evening in a practically comatose condition. Paralysis of the heart is said by the physician to be the direct cause of death following an attack of hydrophobia. During all of Monday Mr. Crisler suffered intense agony and hyoscine was hypodermically injected to quiet him. He was violent part of the time, but his violence was in an effort to get his breath, the choking caused by the paroxysms shutting this off. He had to be restrained by the nurses, Miss Nora Keeney, of Mt. Ayr, and Harry Wiltshire, of Rensselaer, and at night, Vern Crisler, who is a second cousin of the deceased, helped care for him. He suffered intensely up to 4 o'clock in the afternoon and then gradually quieted until 6 o'clock, when he relapsed into a condition of coma and became rigid. He remained this way until the moment of death. He was conscious most of the time until 4 o'clock in the afternoon and fully realized his condition. He begged that some drug might be administered that would hasten his death and relieve his suffering. The funeral will be held in Trinity M. E. church Thursday morning at 10 o'clock, being conducted by Rev. C. L. Harper. Burial will be made in Weston Cemetery. Mr. Crisler was about 63 years of age and leaves a wife and one son, who was a member of the junior class of the Rensselaer high school. Mrs. Benj. Harris is a sister of the deceased."* [26]

Little wonder that for the remainder of his life, Orval never owned a dog and wanted nothing to do with members of the canine family because of his father's sad demise from the bite of a rabid dog. Minnie buried her husband in Weston Cemetery in the town of Rensselaer, just three miles from the farm. His casket was most likely transported from the farm house to the Methodist Episcopal church in Rensselaer where the funeral was held, then to the cemetery by horse-drawn cart. Just two years earlier in 1909 the first automobile hearse had come into existence. However, this new invention was probably not yet available in the small Indiana farm town of Rensselaer. [27]

William was 63 years old at the time of his death, leaving his 52 year-old widow, Minnie and 17 year-old son, Orval. Being a farmer whose income and family support depended on him, William left his family in a dilemma. Orval made the only decision he could and did not return to Rensselaer High School to complete his senior year in the fall following his father's death. He had to take on the responsibilities of an adult and provide support for his mother. William died intestate (without a will) and the administration of his estate in Jasper County in August 1911 revealed an estate worth approximately one thousand dollars in addition to the farmhouse and farm land. An inventory of his belongings revealed household goods worth fifty dollars, four mares, one colt, two cows, and two calves, a boar, a sow and eight piglets, a farm wagon, a carriage, a buggy, a harness and a saddle, and a variety of farm implements including a grain seeder, a cultivator, a disk, two corn planters, a mowing machine and a riding plow breaker. Crops in the field included $250 worth of not yet harvested corn and forty dollars worth of hay. In storage were sixty dollars worth of oats in the granary and forty dollars worth of corn in the corn crib. [28]

Orval's Uncle Ben, husband of his father's sister, Emily Jane Crisler Harris, was a big help to young Orval as he took on the responsibility of being a full-time farmer at the age of seventeen. Orval referred to him as 'ol' Uncle Ben'. Benjamin Harris was known as a very successful and prominent farmer and agriculturist in the Jasper County community of Rensselaer in 1911. Ben served as the administrator for William Crisler's estate following his death, assisting his sister-in-law Minnie and nephew Orval to put William's legal affairs in order. When Ben died only five years later in 1916, he donated land and monies for the formation of the Benjamin Harris Home for Widows and Orphans in the town of Rensselaer. He and his wife, Emily Jane, along with their daughter, Flora, are all buried in Weston Cemetery in Rensselaer.

For the next nine years Orval farmed on the Rensselaer farm providing a living for himself and his mother, Minnie. Sometime in 1920 Orval developed a case of abdominal pain and was hospitalized in the Rensselaer Hospital to have his appendix removed. There he was re-acquainted with his high school classmate Jennie Comer, who by then was a nursing school graduate who was employed at Rensselaer Hospital as a surgical nurse. Orval later said that Jennie took advantage of him when he was at a disadvantage and too sick to defend himself, but apparently the 'love bug' had struck.

Now let us learn about Jennie Comer and find out how she came to be a registered nurse in Rensselaer Hospital in 1920.

Chapter 2

Jennie Mae Comer

Many people would say that Jennie Mae Comer had a rough start in life. She was born on December 1, 1891[29] to her 23 year-old first time mother, Sarah Jane (nicknamed Jennie) Gleason Comer and her 38 year-old father, William Cyrus Comer, in the farm community of Rensselaer, Indiana.

Sarah Jane (Jennie) Gleason (Jennie's mother) circa 1888

William Cyrus Comer (Jennie's father) Date unknown

Sarah Jane and William had been married just over two years when little Jennie was born.[30] Sarah Jane's parents, Oliver J. and Alice Moore Gleason, were residents of the small farm community of Rose Lawn in Newton County, Indiana at the time of their daughter's marriage. The Gleasons had not been supportive of Sarah Jane's marriage to William Comer who was fifteen years her senior. In fact, family legend purports the fact that her parents disowned her for marrying William Comer. Oliver and Alice Gleason moved away from Newton County to a new home in Nunica, Michigan shortly after their daughter's marriage.

William Comer had been married previously and his first wife, Mary Alice Switzer, had died four years earlier leaving two young children, three year old Pearl and five year old Clyde. Without a mother, young Pearl and Clyde were sent to live and be raised by William's two unmarried sisters, Rachel Elizabeth Comer, called Lizzie, and Mary Rebecca Comer, in Rensselaer. Lizzie and Mary were proprietors of a successful boarding house in the town of Rensselaer. At that time it was not expected that a father would (or could) raise young children on his own. William's sisters, Mary and Lizzie Comer, came to his rescue when they agreed to take in his children since they were not married and had no children of their own.

*Rachel Elizabeth and Mary Rebecca Comer
(Jennie's aunts) Date unknown*

After giving birth, Sarah Jane developed childbirth (or puerperal) fever. She was ill for only two weeks before she succumbed to an overwhelming infection just a few months shy of her twenty-fourth birthday.[31]

From *The Rensselaer Republican* published Thursday, December 17, 1891 comes this note:

> *"A sad death which occurred last Tuesday was that of Mrs. Jennie Comer, wife of William Comer, at their residence on Cullen Street, near the old M. E. church. The cause of her death was puerperal fever. Her age was a few weeks less than 24 years. She leaves an infant daughter, aged only two weeks. The funeral was held yesterday afternoon, and at her own request, in the new Baptist church.. She had been married a little over two years, and a member of the Baptist church, three years."*

Now William Comer had three children—Clyde, Pearl and Jennie. How was he going to raise a newborn infant? His sisters, Mary and Lizzie, already were caring for the older children. His only other living female sibling, his married sister Martha Comer Scott, who lived in nearby Benton County,

Indiana had a house full of children (six) of her own. Despite the differences they had with their son-in-law, William Comer, the Gleasons agreed to take the baby and raise it following their daughter's death. Two-week-old Jennie was packed up and sent off two hundred miles to Nunica, Michigan to live with her maternal grandparents, the Gleasons. At the time, grandmother Alice Gleason also had a house full of her own children including fifteen year old Myrtle, twelve year old Bertha, eleven year old Jonathan, ten year old son Birdie, eight year old Oliver, Jr., five year old William, three year old Edna, and baby Orth, only three months old when his Aunt Sarah Jane died following childbirth. Alice would give birth to another daughter, Violet in 1896. Undoubtedly, the older daughters, Myrtle and Bertha were asked to help with new family member, Jennie.

Childbirth fever was fairly common in the 1890s. Statistics from that time indicate that one in twenty women in a hospital giving birth would die, forty percent of the deaths were due to infection. It would take another forty years to improve those statistics because the cause of childbirth fever was controversial within the medical community and antibiotics were not yet available. We know today that it is a serious infection of the female reproductive organs that is a result of trauma to those tissues during childbirth that often leads to septicemia (blood poisoning) and death from organ failure. The infection, caused most commonly by the bacteria strains of staphylococcus and streptococcus, was often carried on the dirty hands and medical instruments of doctors and midwives. Sadly, puerperal fever was virtually unknown prior to the development of 'lying in' (maternity) hospitals for women in the mid 1800s. Prior to that, most women gave birth at home and did not suffer from childbirth fever. In 1879, Louis Pasteur showed that streptococcus was present in the blood of women with childbirth fever but physicians were slow to understand how to prevent it. It was not until the 1930s that appropriate specific cures for childbirth fever would be developed and the death rate lowered significantly.[32] We do not know whether or not Sarah Jane gave birth at home with a physician or midwife in attendance or whether she was in the hospital at the time. Her death certificate does not specify that information.

Interestingly, no birth certificate for Jennie Comer has been found in Jasper County. Since Indiana state law did not require registration of births until 1907 it is likely that Jennie's birth was never registered in Jasper County. Understandably, there must have been considerable confusion in the Comer household at that time. William was dealing with the arrangements for first an ill wife and a newborn baby, then the funeral arrangements following his young wife's untimely death. We do have the newspaper article announcing Sarah Jane's death that gives us Jennie's birth information. Another interesting fact regarding Jennie's birth is that she was not given a middle name.

Later in life, as she was preparing to graduate from high school, she would decide to give herself a middle name and called herself Jennie Mae. When she applied for a social security number in 1963, she is listed as Jennie Mae Crisler.

As Jennie grew up in Nunica, Michigan in her grandparent's home she apparently had minimal contact with her father, William Comer. William, a carpenter by training, had left Rensselaer and moved to nearby Hendricks County, Indiana were he married in 1894 for a third time to a Quaker woman, Mary Ann Poor. He lived most of the rest of his life in Hendricks County working as a house carpenter returning to Rensselaer only after Mary Ann's death in 1920.[33]

He died in Rensselaer in 1926 at age 73[34] and is buried in Weston Cemetery next to his sisters, Lizzie and Mary, and his daughter, Pearl and her husband, George Myer.[35]

His obituary when it appeared in the Rensselaer Republican on December 31, 1926:

> *"Wm. C. Comer Succumbs to Long Illness*
> *Aged Resident Expires at Jasper County Hospital: Funeral Service Saturday P.M.*
>
> *William C. Comer, an old and respected resident of this city, died at the Jasper county hospital at 3:30 o'clock Thursday afternoon, his death resulting after a long illness from a complication of diseases and twenty-two weeks after he entered the hospital.*
>
> *Mr. Comer was born in Jasper county February 7, 1853, the son of John E. and Mazilla Comer. His boyhood and early manhood were spent in his native country. When a young man he took up the carpenter's trade which he followed throughout his active life. Twenty five years or more ago he went to Hendricks county, residing near Danville, where he remained until six years ago, at which time his wife died and he came to Rensselaer to make his home with his daughter and sisters.*
>
> *The deceased was thrice married. His first wife was Miss Alice Switzer of this county, who died many years ago. His second wife, Miss Jennie Gleason, a Jasper county lady, also preceded him to the grave. His third wife, Mary Pore of Hendricks county, died December 30, 1920, exactly six years to the day on which he received his final summons.*
>
> *Mr. Comer is survived by three children, Clyde Comer of Winchester, Indiana, Miss Pearl Comer of this city, and Mrs. Jennie Crisler of Rochester, Indiana, the former two the fruits of*

> *his first marriage and the latter of his second marriage. Three sisters also survive him. They are Misses Elizabeth and Mary Comer of this city and Mrs. A. B. Scott of Oxford.*
>
> *Mr. Comer was an unassuming Christian gentleman, kind and considerate to those about him. Early in life he united with the Friends church, taking out his membership in the church at Hadley, Indiana. He remained constant to that faith throughout his life.*
>
> *The funeral services will be held at two o'clock Saturday afternoon at the Comer house on S. Cullen Street. Interment will be made in Weston cemetery."*[36]

As of this writing, Sarah Jane's burial location has not been found. Logically she would have been buried close to her death locale but research in Rensselaer, the surrounding Jasper and Newton County locale and even the Ottawa County, Michigan area where her parents were living in 1891, has proved futile in finding her resting place. She is most likely buried near Rensselaer since her obituary indicates she was buried on December 16, 1891, the day following her death. [37] She is most likely buried in an unmarked grave in the city of Rensselaer or the surrounding Jasper County area.

William Comer's family had lived in Jasper County, Indiana since the 1830s. His father, William Ellis Comer, was an early settler and purchaser of land from the federal government through the land grant program in 1838.[38] His ancestors also were farmers that may have traced their ancestry to Germany. In "A Standard History of Jasper and Newton Counties Indiana" a passage indicates that:

> *"the progenitor of the Comer family in America was Jesse Comer, a Hessian German, who came to America with the Hessian troops during the Revolutionary War. He soon became convinced of the justice of the colonist's cause, and like many of his fellow soldiers, deserted from the army of King George and subsequently became a loyal American citizen. The particular manner in which he accomplished his desertion is interesting. He had long had in mind the idea of the step he was to take, and in order to carry out his plan practiced imitating the grunt of a hog, in the meantime stirring the leaves and grass with a stick to represent the noise made by that animal in going about. When he felt that he had his imitation to perfection, and at a time when the troops were encamped upon the banks of a river, probably the Brandywine, he put his plan into execution. At the challenge of the sentinel: "Who goes there?" his answer was a grunt, accompanied by the stirring of the leaves and grass,*

which completely deceived the sentinel, who ejaculated: "It's only a hog." When Mr. Comer rolled over into the river, the sentinel realized another soldier was endeavoring to desert, and he and his comrades all along the bank began firing at every suspicious sound, but by diving and swimming Mr. Comer eventually succeeded in reaching the opposite bank where he found friends and safety."[39]

Many Comer ancestors including William Comer's parents, John Ellis Comer and his wife Mazilla DeWitt (or Daywitt) Comer and his Comer grandfather, Jesse Comer are all buried in Jasper County, Indiana. John Ellis and his wife Mazilla are buried in Weston Cemetery in Rensselaer.[40] Jesse Comer, grandson of the Hessian soldier, also named Jesse, is buried in Barkley Cemetery behind the Barkley Methodist Episcopal Church in rural Jasper County, northeast of Rensselaer. [41]Jesse Comer was the first person to be buried in Barkley Cemetery when he died in 1844.

Oliver Gleason, Jennie's grandfather, was a Civil War veteran, having served as a private in the Union Army in the 4th Illinois Cavalry in the years 1864-1865.[42] He enlisted at Kankakee County, Illinois which is just across the border from neighboring Newton and Jasper Counties, Indiana when he was residing in Lake Village, Newton County, Indiana.[43] Following his military experience he returned home to Indiana where he took up farming as his occupation. Oliver and his wife, Alice Moore, had both been born in Canada.[44] [45] Both of their families had moved to Canada in the years following the Revolutionary War. Genealogical research indicates that the Gleasons probably were of English descent having come to Massachusetts in the early 1600s [46] while the Moore family was of German or Dutch descent.

Jennie Comer lived with her Gleason grandparents in Crockery Township just outside the small town of Nunica, Michigan in the southwest corner of the state during her early childhood years. Her grandfather, Oliver Gleason, was a farmer. Grandmother Alice was a mother, grandmother and homemaker. Nunica was a small town of about four hundred inhabitants during the 1890s when Jennie lived there. The town of Nunica, first settled in 1855, grew up around the Detroit, Grand Haven and Milwaukee Railroad depot and became a logging town in the period of 1855-1880. The railroad through Nunica, however, did not last until Jennie's arrival in town in 1891. Its tracks had been torn out around 1880 when a fire swept through town burning down the railroad depot station along with several other town businesses.

During the decade of the 1890s when Jennie lived in Nunica with her Gleason grandparents the town was a prosperous rural community, despite the demise of the railroad. Businesses included several general stores including one owned and operated by Oliver Gleason's cousin,

Jonathan Gleason Westover, a creamery, a mill, a combination pharmacy/ post office, as well as a doctor's office and a veterinary office. Other businesses included a coal yard, a farm implement store and a J. H. Heinz Pickle Factory. Three churches, one Methodist Episcopal, one German Evangelical, and one Congregational, one school, and a town hall were also in the downtown area, along with the Odd Fellows Lodge. The historical publication '*The Crockery Collection*' provides an interesting insight into small town life in 1900 when Jennie lived in Nunica. A grocery wagon owned by Mr. Bekins had a regular route in and around Nunica bringing groceries to his clients. His wagon was a cumbersome looking vehicle "not unlike a railroad box car". [47] It had no rubber tires, only wide steel-rimmed wagon wheels. Mr. Bekins carried many grocery supplies, sewing needs and other sundries found in a country general store. It was drawn by two draft-type horses and only came when the roads were in favorable condition. If a farmer's wife did not have ready cash, Mr. Bekins would accept fresh dairy butter or eggs in exchange for her purchase. The roads in and around Nunica were unpaved in the 1890s. In 1897, the major road through town got a layer of gravel but the roads in town would not be paved until automobiles demanded it after the turn of the twentieth century. [48]

When Nunica was first platted by Henry Ernst in the mid 1800s, lumbering was the major industry of the district. At the time there were some very good farms and many of the land owners combined farming with the cutting of logs, peeling tanbark and other forest land occupations. With the passing of the years and the clearing of the land, farming and stock-raising became more prevalent. Many farmers also supplemented their usual crops with maple sugaring for maple syrup, berry production as well as fruit trees, apple and peach.

Village life in Nunica can give us an idea of what Jennie and her Gleason family experienced in the 1890s. According to the Crockery Collection, "Saturdays were special to the folks living in the country."[49] That was the big day to go shopping in town and visit with friends. The hardware store in town was a local gathering place where some of the men gathered to talk and settle all the problems of the world. The old stove was the popular spot and the coal scuttle served as the spittoon for the tobacco chewers. Oliver Gleason probably frequented the Pickett Implement Store in downtown Nunica. Pickett's was a dependable repair and parts supply store and also sold hay, straw, binder twine, and fertilizer in addition to farm machinery. Alice would have frequented one of the three general stores in town but probably for just a few staples like coffee, tea, salt, pepper and some spices. Most businesses on Main Street in Nunica had a bench out in front for use of the public to rest or visit with friends. When the weather got cold everyone moved inside around the wood stove.

Oliver and Alice probably had their mail delivered by rural delivery via horse drawn wagon. Telephones would not come to Nunica until 1897 and we don't know whether or not the Gleasons were telephone customers at the time that Jennie was living with them.

At that time, activities for young people were simple and usually close to home. Summer time brought church socials, buggy rides and picnics. During the cold winter months the young people especially liked taking sleigh rides in the snow and ice skating on the frozen ponds and lakes in the area. Several farmers in the area surrounding Nunica had ice houses that they filled with ice cut from nearby Spring Lake each winter. In addition to keeping their perishable foods cold the ice was used for the fun event of home-made ice cream, a real treat in the days before refrigeration. When the farmers banded together to saw the huge blocks of ice to fill their ice houses, it became a community event. The women furnished hot coffee and home-made donuts followed by lavish noon meals. Popping corn was a must and folks enjoyed cracking and eating nuts. According to Sherman Gleason, a second cousin to Jennie, and a lifelong resident of Crockery Township, every household in Crockery Township had a dozen store-bought nut picks for the job of cracking nuts, a job usually given to the older children. In addition to popped corn and nuts, winter-time fun involved candy making, taffy pulling, and quick-made snow ice cream. According to Sherman Gleason, snow ice cream was delicious with vanilla or lemon flavoring and sweet cream mixed in the clean snow. After mixing, the snow ice cream was set outdoors to freeze harder. The children would entertain themselves playing dominoes, checkers, 'old cat', tic-tac-toe and several other homemade games. Adults would play cards, tell stories and gossip about who would plant what the following spring.

We have no records of the exact types of farm products that were produced by Oliver Gleason on his farm but by looking at the information from Crockery Township data we can make some good guesses. In 1873 the following crops were produced in Ottawa County, Michigan—wheat, corn, potatoes, other grains, hay, wool, butter and maple sugar. By 1900 the mechanical age of farming had become well established. The old single furrow walking plow had given way to larger riding plows with a three horse hitch which Oliver probably used. Mowing machines had been in use for many years, and new side delivery hay-rakes combined with newly developed hay loaders made haying operation much easier. At its height around 1900 Crockery Township boasted over one hundred active farm operations.[50] Oliver Gleason's farm was one.

The school building that Jennie and her aunts and uncles would have attended was built in 1875 by John Westover, a first cousin of Jennie's grandfather, Oliver J. Gleason. In the late 1800s there were two teachers. Mary Smith taught the younger children, 'Judge' Taylor taught the older ones. Judge Taylor acquired his nickname 'Judge' because he also served his community as a justice of the peace. In the 1890s there were fall terms, winter terms, and spring terms. Boys old enough to work attended the winter term only. Male teachers were often hired for that term. There were no compulsory school attendance laws at the time. When Jennie attended Nunica School there were four classrooms, two up and two down. The lower rooms held Kindergarten through second and third grade, and fourth and fifth grades. Upstairs held the sixth through eighth grades and the ninth and tenth grades. Sliding down the stairway banister was one of the favorite tricks of the upstairs students, much to the annoyance of their teachers. Each classroom was heated by a coal burning stove. Bathroom facilities consisted of an outhouse behind the school. There were no hot lunches and each student brought their own lunch in a tin lunch bucket, or in some cases, an empty syrup pail. Children would have been expected to walk to and from school each day.

Teachers were expected to not only teach, but also to maintain order, keep the fire burning in cold weather, sweep the floors and keep the building clean, all for less than $45 per month. The teachers, usually women because they could be hired at a lower wage, would often board out among the various property owners living in the district, receiving part of their salary in meals and lodging. According to a history of Crockery Township "most of the early settlers in this part of the country were Eastern people, well educated themselves" [51] who understood the value of education for their children. Schools were one of the first things built in Crockery Township and were known as some of the best in the area of southwest Michigan.

The church that Jennie, her grandparents and her other relatives would have attended was the Nunica Methodist Church located on South Street in Nunica. It, too, was built by John Westover, a Gleason relation. [52] Men of the community had donated material and labor for the building of the church in 1874. Timbers were hewn from trees on a local farm and construction was a community effort.

Jennie was only seven and a half years old when her forty-six year old grandmother, Alice, became ill and died. Alice's obituary which appeared in the Grand Haven Daily Tribune on March 10, 1899 explains the suddenness of her death:

> *"Mrs. Oliver Gleason, Sr., was found dead upon the floor of her home, Thursday, March 2 by her little son upon returning from school. The two youngest were with her, a mother-*

less granddaughter, six or seven years, and her own, two and one-half years. Examination proved a fatty heart and cancerous liver. She had not fully recovered from a serious attack early in January. She was the mother of ten children, seven of whom survive her. She leaves a husband, mother, five brothers, two sisters and a host of relatives and friends. Funeral Sunday at the M. E. Church".[53]

Note the mention above of a "motherless granddaughter", undoubtedly Jennie Comer. The two and half year old was her Uncle Orth Henry Gleason.

We don't know much about what happened following this sad death, but from census records we do know that Jennie went to live at least for a short time with her Aunt Myrtle Gleason Shaw and Myrtle's husband Elam Mason Shaw in Crockery Township, Michigan. When the 1900 U.S. Federal Census was enumerated on June 1, 1900, Jennie was living with her Aunt Myrtle and Uncle Elam.[54] Twenty three year old Myrtle had just given birth to her first child, a son, Richard, in January 1899 when her mother (and Jennie's grandmother) died in March 1899. Later in life Jennie told her family that as she was growing up in the Gleason household she went by the name Jennie Gleason and actually thought that was her correct name. However, in the 1900 census we find her listed as Jennie Comer, age eight, niece of Myrtle Shaw. Jennie also told her family that when her grandfather, Oliver Gleason, wanted to re-marry, his second wife, Miss Ida Herington, wanted nothing to do with her and that is why she was sent back to Rensselaer, Indiana to live with her two aunts, Lizzie and Mary Comer.

Jennie recounted how she was put on the interurban train (the Grand Rapids, Grand Haven and Muskegon Railroad) by herself in Nunica to travel to Chicago where she had to change trains and stations to catch the Monon route train to Rensselaer. We have to make an educated guess to determine how old Jennie was when she took this trip to return to her Indiana relatives. Since her grandfather Oliver remarried in November 1900, just a year and a half after the death of his first wife, Alice, we can guess that Jennie probably returned to Indiana sometime between June and November 1900.

The interurban railroads were examples of a mode of transportation devised in the 1890s to provide transportation where steam railroads were not yet providing service.[55] The Grand Rapids, Grand Haven and Muskegon railroad had unique orange-colored cars and provided service to the residents of Crockery Township during a time when they were ready to move beyond the horse and buggy and prior to the arrival of the Model T. The Monon route ran from Chicago's Dearborn station to Rensselaer on its way to Louisville, Kentucky.

Once back in Rensselaer, Jennie settled into the Comer Boarding House on South Cullen Street in Rensselaer with her Aunt Mary and Aunt Lizzie and her half brother, Clyde Comer, and half sister, Pearl Comer.

Comer Boarding House on S. Cullen Street in Rensselaer,
IN as it appeared in 2007

In 1900, Clyde was twenty years old and was working as a telephone operator in Rensselaer. Pearl was seventeen years old and was listed as a student in the 1900 census enumeration.[56] According to Jennie, the expectations of Mary and Lizzie were that their nieces and nephew would work in return for their care in the Comer house.

The boarding house of the 1900s reflected the first stage of the growth of large cities (and apparently smaller ones as well). Young men coming off the farm and looking for work in town needed some kind of sheltering environment. For a reasonable amount boarders could find a room (though not always private), meals and sometimes laundry. The typical boarding house keeper was often a married, middle-class woman who needed to earn an income. This often put her in contradiction to the social ideal of the times. By assuming the male role and earning money she was considered by many of her peers to be a shameful embarrassment. Working at home and capitalizing on her domestic skills, she did not seem quite as scandalous to her community as she might have been working in a more public factory, office, or shop and may have been able to maintain something of her social position.[57]

However, keeping a boarding house was no easy task. Boarding house proprietors were kept busy from dawn to dusk and it is no wonder that Mary and Lizzie welcomed the help of three young people. While Clyde was employed outside the house as a telephone operator, Jennie and her half-sister Pearl were expected to perform housework for their keep. Jennie would later tell her children about having to stand on a chair so that she could reach the sink to wash the dishes following meals for the boarders.

Jennie was able to continue her education and she attended the public schools in Rensselaer to complete grammar (elementary) school and high school. She graduated from Rensselaer High School in 1912 at the age of twenty. She went to school during the day but then helped out before and after school at the Comer Boarding House. The Comer House was, according to Aunt Lizzie's obituary when it appeared in the *Rensselaer Republican* in 1933, an extremely popular boarding house known for its excellent management and home-like atmosphere that enjoyed liberal patronage. Aunt Lizzie, as she was known to her neighbors, was a "quiet and unobtrusive character, generous and at all times thoughtful of those in less fortunate circumstances than she. The many kindnesses she daily bestowed upon those about her, the helping hand which she so freely extended to all and the beautiful Christian life she led made her an outstanding character that Rensselaer people generally will greatly miss."[58] Rachel's sister, Mary Comer, was described in her obituary in 1935 as "one of the city's sweetest and most admired characters. Her life was one that brought good cheer and the atmosphere of her home was one of marked hospitality."[59]

We don't know specifically what types of clothing Jennie wore during childhood since there is only one photograph of her as a young child. The first known photograph we have of her was taken when she was about twelve years old.

Jennie Comer age 12, circa 1903

We can also make assumptions about her apparel from what we know of what others were wearing at that time. During the 1890s women's dresses reached the floor and required yards of fabric. Corsets, chemises and pantaloons were part of each woman's underclothing usually made from fine linen, silk or muslin.[60] Children's apparel was usually a smaller copy of the adult clothing. Most women made their own clothes following standardized patterns provided by companies named McCalls and Buttericks. Apparel was sewn at home on manual treadle sewing machines. Professional dressmakers would have used the same patterns. Seamstresses bought their fabric and supplies at their local dry goods store. Following the turn of century, well-made ready-to-wear clothing made its appearance. Women may have ordered some of their clothing from the Sears, Roebuck and Company catalog. A new fashion innovation was the shirtwaist, a blouse designed to be worn with a skirt. By 1905 the Sears, Roebuck catalogue offered one hundred and fifty variations of it, from a plain lawn version costing thirty-nine cents to one made from taffeta for almost seven dollars. Following the death of England's Queen Victoria in 1901, there was a definite decline in the formality of clothing for both genders. Long skirts started to raise, first to just the top of the lady's boot, later higher. In the first decade of the 1900s no fashionable woman would have left her house without a hat on. Many single women worked as dressmakers and milliners to support themselves.[61]

As Jennie approached adulthood she had a major decision to make. She was twenty years old when she graduated from Rensselaer High School, two years past the customary graduation date for most high school students today as in 1912. We can assume that because she had to move from her grandparent's home in 1899 to her Aunt Myrtle's home and then to her Comer aunts' home back in Rensselaer, her education timetable was slightly delayed. When she graduated from high school her desire was to become a registered nurse and she was ready to head off to Chicago for nursing school at Wesley Memorial Hospital, ninety miles away. However, she knew that the expectation of her Aunt Mary and Aunt Lizzie was that she would stay on and help out in the boarding house. At this point Mary was 62 years old and Lizzie was 65 years old, certainly at a time when they were anticipating being able to slow down a little and let their young nieces, Pearl and Jennie, and their nephew Clyde, take over some of the responsibility of running the Comer Boarding House. This was long before the arrival of social security insurance and single, unmarried women had to make their own livings or depend on their families to support them. They felt that Jennie, Pearl and Clyde needed to pay them back for the years they spent supporting them during their growing up years.

Jennie made the tough decision of a risk taker and chose to attend nursing school in Chicago, leaving her disappointed aunts along with her half sister and half brother in Rensselaer. Jennie would later tell her children that her Aunt Mary and Aunt Lizzie disowned her for leaving Rensselaer and the Comer Boarding House. The wills of Mary and Lizzie filed in the Jasper County Courthouse in Rensselaer bear this truth out since Jennie was not mentioned in either of their wills.

Off to the big city of Chicago, Jennie enrolled in the three year diploma nursing program at Wesley Memorial Hospital (affiliated with Northwestern University) in 1912. Applicants to the school of nursing were required to be of " good Christian character, between the ages of 20 and 32, inclusive, and must have completed at least two years of high school work and preference for applicants with a higher education is given." [62] Following completion of a brief one page application, prospective nurses were advised to provide a personal letter giving their reasons for taking up the work and also provide letters of reference from their pastor and physician. Jennie's first class at nursing school commenced on October 3, 1912. Following the successful completion of the three month long probationary period in early January 1913, she was given credit for the three month's work and accepted as a full-fledged pupil of the school. [63]

While at Wesley, Jennie lived at the Harris Home for Nurses located at 2342 Dearborn Street in Chicago, one block north of the Wesley Memorial Hospital. The home was a four-story brick building with accommodations for eighty nurses, most in single rooms. Fees included a laboratory fee of twenty dollars for the entire three year course and twelve dollars for textbooks including Chemistry, Bacteriology, Obstetrics, Anatomy, Nursing and Materia Medica (Pharmacology). These were the only fees. Room, board and the laundry of the student uniforms was provided to each student. In return for this fairly inexpensive education, even by the standards of 1912, the student nurse provided considerable labor within the hospital wards. Jennie would later discourage her eldest daughter, Virginia, from entering nursing as a profession because of this fact. She felt nursing students were used too much for 'grunt labor'. She also related to her granddaughter and later nurse Leslie, that nurses at that time were not even allowed to take a patient's blood pressure. That was always the responsibility of a physician. Certainly the responsibilities of nurses have changed in the almost one hundred years since Jennie was a nursing student at Wesley.

Probationary students were required to provide their own uniforms with very specific guidelines and instructions given on fabric and style. The school of nursing's brochure for that time period specified that aprons made otherwise would need to be altered at the probationer's expense. They also needed to bring with them "plenty of underclothing, all marked with the owner's name in indelible ink, two laundry bags, 24 inches by 36 inches in size, scissors, napkin ring, fountain pen, and watch". They were required to wear high black leather shoes with rubber heels (oxfords could be worn in summer). "Nurses will receive uniforms and cuffs from the hospital during their freshmen year only. In their junior and senior years they will furnish their own uniforms, under the direction of the school's principal." They were provided an allowance of four dollars per month in their junior year and six dollars per month in their senior year for the purchase of uniforms and textbooks. They were required to have been vaccinated (probably a smallpox vaccination) and have been to a dentist for a dental exam and appropriate dental care prior to enrollment. [64]

Daily attendance at chapel in the hospital library each morning was required. And although church attendance was not compulsory, it was strongly encouraged. Rules for the Harris Home give us an idea of how regulated their lives were:

- The rising bell is rung at 5:45 A.M.
- First breakfast is served at 6:30 A.M.
- Second breakfast is served at 7:30 A.M.
- Prayers in library at 7:00 A.M.

- Day nurses go on duty at 7:00 A.M.
- Each pupil nurse is expected to keep her own room in order and to observe the rules of domestic hygiene
- Night nurses must be in their rooms at 9:00 A.M. and may not go out until 5:00 P.M. without permission

As one might guess from its name, Wesley Memorial Hospital was associated with the Methodist church. Its school of nursing dated from 1888 with the first three graduates in 1890. In the early 1900s dramatic changes were taking place in medical care resulting in unprecedented growth in both hospitals and nursing schools. Between 1900 and 1910, over sixteen hundred new hospitals opened in this country and the number of training schools for nurses rose from 432 to 1,120. No longer "pest-houses" as in the past, hospitals were beginning to be viewed as places of healing. With this growth, physicians and hospital administrators began tapping the lucrative income potential of student nurses. Patients were charged directly for the services of student nurses (both on the wards and for private duty). In the year preceding Jennie's enrollment at Wesley, income from the nursing services provided by Wesley nursing students totaled more than $42,000.[65]

More patients meant the need for more nurses and nursing schools. Wesley reported that in 1903 it had more than four hundred applicants for just fifty-five openings. However, the strenuous work involved did take a toll on its students. Long hours and constant exposure to illness and disease exacted a heavy toll. Sick days had to be made up at the end of the course, so it was not uncommon for students who had already graduated to stay on several months until their term expired.

The probationary period for Jennie and her classmates was the ultimate test of a student's physical and emotional strength. The probies were thrust into an environment of strict discipline, intense scrutiny, hard work, and the ever-present perils of "on-the-job" training. Not every student survived the ordeal. At Wesley nearly half of all probationers were dismissed as "incompetent, physically unfit, or lacking the stability of character" for a career in nursing. Some left voluntarily rather than accept the menial and distasteful duties assigned to them. Others found the reality of training sorely at odds with their romanticized notions of nursing. Those completing the probationary period were "rewarded" with permission to wear the school uniform and a monthly allowance to cover expenses of textbooks and laboratory equipment. Students were required to sign a contract agreeing to remain for the duration of the course, to subordinate themselves to the staff, and "faithfully obey the rules" of the school and the hospital.

On average, student nurses were assigned to night duty for three months out of the year. While assigned to night duty, students were required to remain in their rooms from 9 A.M. to 4 P.M. The shift began at 7:30 P.M. and ended at 7:30 A.M. with three hours off. While on duty students were not only responsible for their patients, but also housekeeping duties, cooking, and filling prescriptions in the pharmacy. Constant repetition of routine tasks performed the "hospital way" was stressed. Classes and lectures were held every day but Sunday. Students were to be in their room by 10 P.M. with 'lights out' strictly enforced half an hour later.

An interesting insight into the students at Wesley can be seen in a description of the Wesley's Loving Cup. Although students worked long hours, they occasionally found time for some good-natured (if not rowdy fun). The senior class was custodian of a cowbell which was rung frequently during graduation week both in the hospital and at the nurses' home. The spine-shuddering sound was the signal for the juniors to engage in Amazonian combat for possession of the cowbell. Students would briefly excuse themselves from patients' bedsides in pursuit of their prize. The spirit of the event rose to such a fevered pitch that some students slept in their corsets in order to more quickly answer the call to conflict. These goings-on created so much disruption that finally the officers of the hospital and school gave the Class of 1910 the responsibility for arriving at a peaceful solution to the annual contest. A senior student, a professional golfer, offered one of her many trophies as an appropriate endowment to the junior class and a new tradition was begun. Each year at the Senior Recognition Dinner, the graduates drank mulberry juice from the cup before presenting it to the juniors with "esteem and fellowship" rather than through raucous rivalry. Jennie would have missed the rowdy fun of previous classes since her graduating class of 1915 would have participated in the replacement recognition with the Wesley Loving Cup. [66]

Following three full years in Chicago, Jennie along with twenty-six other classmates became a graduate of Wesley Memorial Hospital School of Nursing. Her graduation photograph reveal her in a nurse's uniform and cap designating her as a graduate of Wesley Memorial Hospital.

Jennie Mae Comer . Nursing graduate 1915

Jennie would maintain the friendships she made while at Wesley over many years of her adult life. A fun photograph shows a group of her nurse friends several years following their graduation.

Wesley Hospital friends. Jennie is in back row, second from left

Her daughter Virginia remembers several class mates including Helen Jones, Emma Hansen and Gladys Grant, close friends of Jennie who she stayed in contact with for many years following graduation. Gladys would send Jennie her niece's hand-me-down clothing and Virginia thought she was "queen of the hill" when she got to wear them. Helen Jones was known to Jennie and Orval's children as 'Aunt Helen'.

With her nursing degree in hand, Jennie was ready to move on but did not immediately return to Rensselaer. She took her first nursing position in Kankakee, Illinois, just over the state line from Indiana, less than fifty miles away from Rensselaer. A few years later she would return to Rensselaer and work as a surgical nurse and radiology technician at Rensselaer Hospital. It is while she was working at Rensselaer Hospital in 1920 that she became reacquainted with a former high school classmate, Orval Crisler. Orval was suffering from appendicitis and was a hospital patient following removal of his appendix when the two met again.

Chapter 3

Crisler Couple—The Early Years

Little is known about the courtship of Jennie and Orval. We know that they met while both were high school students at Rensselaer High School and became re-acquainted when Orval was hospitalized at Rensselaer Hospital for emergency appendectomy surgery when both were in their late 20s. At that time Jennie was working as a surgical nurse and she was Orval's nurse during his hospitalization. Orval was a farmer supporting himself and his widowed mother on their small farm outside of Rensselaer. Later Orval would jokingly say that Jennie caught him during a weak moment and he couldn't defend himself. But certainly he was only teasing because it was a marriage that would last more than sixty-five years. The two fell in love and decided to marry.

About this time in the United States a major change was taking place—the old-fashioned period of courtship was being replaced by a more modern period of 'dating'. Courtship was the traditional dating period before engagement and marriage. During courtship a couple dated to get to know each other and decide if there would be an engagement. Courtship usually was a public affair, done in public and with family approval. The couple would be chaperoned at all times. After the turn of the twentieth century, the courtship pattern was giving way to a more informal pattern of contact between young people, possibly due to the freedom provided by the automobile and this was probably true for Orval and Jennie since Orval was the proud owner of a Maxwell Touring car.

We know that Orval presented Jennie with a diamond engagement ring and the wedding date was set for October. Fashions in wedding rings were changing as rapidly as dress fashions. Matching engagement and wedding bands were the order of the day. The high set diamond solitaire gave way to square or lace mounts similar to Jennie's. Platinum or white gold were preferred over the traditional yellow color.[67]

Jennie and Orval decided to marry in a small ceremony with only a few family members who would serve as their witnesses. They applied for a wedding license in Rensselaer at the Jasper County courthouse on September 30, 1920.[68] The following day Orval, Jennie, her older half sister Pearl Comer and Orval's mother, Minnie Crisler, made a road trip to Lafayette, Indiana, about forty-five miles away, in Orval's Maxwell Touring Sedan for their wedding. Their nuptials were conducted at the home of Methodist Episcopal minister, Reverend Edward W. Strecker and his wife Elizabeth. Pastor Strecker had only recently moved from Rensselaer where he had served as the pastor of the Methodist Episcopal Church in Rensselaer to a new church in Lafayette. Pearl and Minnie, along with Mrs. Strecker, served as witnesses to the young couple's ceremony.

Following their wedding ceremony the newlyweds traveled further south to French Lick Springs in southern Indiana for their honeymoon. French Lick was a bustling tourist resort in 1920. The town of French Lick, named because of the rich mineral springs, which attracted animals that flocked there to lick the water and wet rocks, became known as "French Lick" during the days when most of Indiana's inhabitants were native Indians. During the 1800s and early 1900s visitors were drawn to the healing waters of the many springs at French Lick where a resort with opulent architecture and décor was built and became well-known. French Lick would later draw many famous Americans including fighter Joe Lewis, composer Irving Berlin, and President Franklin D. Roosevelt. Orval and Jennie may also have visited nearby tourist attractions including the Lincoln Boyhood Memorial where Abraham Lincoln lived for fourteen years of his childhood, magnificent caves at Marengo Cave National Monument, the Hoosier National Forest, and the West Baden Springs National Historic Landmark, another resort hotel which in 1902 was named the eighth wonder of the world.[69]

The newly married couple did not have a fancy church wedding nor do any professional photos of their wedding exist. A photograph taken by the bride is the only known photo of that special time in their lives. Jennie had become interested in photography and had purchased a Kodak camera prior to her marriage. Clever rigging of a string to the camera's shutter allowed her to take this photograph at French Lick during the first few days of their marriage. Kodak's Brownie camera had come out in 1900 and was available to amateur photographers at a cost of one dollar.

Orval and Jennie at French Lick State Park October 1920

Back on the farm in Rensselaer the young couple started their married life together living with Orval's widowed mother, Minnie. Orval continued farming while Jennie shared the many household responsibilities with her new mother-in-law. Orval used horses to cultivate his fields and his daughter, Virginia, remembers that he had three large draft horses. Nell and Topsy were used routinely for most field work.

Orval Crisler plowing his farm in Rensselaer, Indiana circa 1925

Nell and Topsy were joined by Sam when Orval needed a three horse team for some of the heavier duty work. There were three dairy cows and a bull that were bestowed names but whose names are now forgotten. There were also a few pigs, but after a run-in with an angry sow, Jennie insisted that Orval get rid of the pigs. Chickens were primarily Jennie's responsibility and the eggs she collected were mostly for home use. Any extra eggs were carried into town and sold. Jennie even had an incubator in her basement on the farm where she raised her own chicks. This required regular attention to turning the eggs on a routine basis several times daily just as a mother hen would do while the eggs were incubating.

Orval grew much of his fodder for his stock of horses and cows. His year was punctuated by the annual rhythm of loading spreaders and manuring fields in late winter, plowing, disking and planting in the spring, cultivating in summer and harvesting in the autumn, as well as haying whenever the fields were ready. In the evening cows had to be brought back from the pasture or let into the barn for milking.

Orval Crisler on his back porch after a hard day on the farm circa 1920

A typical day for Orval began at sun up (or earlier in the winter months). Before breakfast he would have been out in his barn to feed his stock and milk his cows. The milk, once collected, would have been the responsibility of Jennie or Minnie to process for home use, to separate the cream and to make cheese and buttermilk. Some was sold in town and Virginia remembers milk cans being set out at the end of the farm lane for pick up. While Orval was out in the barn, Jennie would have been in the house making breakfast. She would have used the wood burning cook stove in the kitchen to make Orval the breakfast he liked consisting of eggs, breakfast meat, well-toasted bread (he like his bread toasted until it was almost burnt - "burnt offering"), and coffee. Bread was toasted by spearing a piece of bread on a fork and toasting it carefully over the open flame of the wood stove.

After morning chores, there was the daily routine of mucking out stables and barns, cleaning out pig pens and chicken coops and a myriad of other tasks, depending on the season. Farmers like Orval usually handled the large animals, fixed the farm machinery when it broke down and did the plowing and the planting. Minnie and Jennie would have helped with the hoeing, weeding and crop harvesting, care of the chickens, the kitchen garden, as well as all of the household chores.

But many changes were coming to Midwest farms at this time that would impact the lives of Orval, Jennie and Minnie. Electricity was making its way to the rural areas of the country and the Crisler farm in Indiana was no exception. Throughout the country in 1912, sixteen percent of the population lived in houses with electric lights and sixty-three percent did so in 1927.[70] Electric lights replaced the dimmer, smelly, dirty and dangerous open flames of kerosene lights. They also eliminated cleaning lamp parts, snipping ragged wicks, and cleaning soot left by the lamps. At some point in the late 1910s Orval installed a Delco generator for electricity on the farm. Virginia remembers that Orval was always interested in having the latest technological advances and even though the generator was far from being an inexpensive addition the Crislers were one of the first in their area to have a generator. Although electricity transmission lines were common in the urban areas of this country in the 1920s, the rural areas were slower to be electrified. Unlike Orval, many farmers were reluctant to embrace electrical power. Neighborly persuasion was often needed to obtain enough new customers to support and justify an electrical line in the rural areas. In the meantime, farmers like Orval bought their own generators to produce electricity for use on the farm. "In times past, the farmer who owned a Delco generator was living high on the hog".[71] In 1941 a Delco generator cost $310. Imagine what it cost in 1920. In most homes the Delco generator was used initially for generating power for light, and later for the radio, refrigerator, and the iron. The Crislers would not have a radio, an icebox or an electric iron until after they left the farm. The Delco Company reported that its production of generators peaked between 1916 and 1946.

On the Crisler farm the generator was set up in the shed in the backyard. There, a bank of batteries consisting of sixteen jars, a row of eight on one shelf and another row of eight on the next shelf produced direct current (unlike the alternating current that we currently use today). An engine powered by gasoline generated the electricity. A motor charged the batteries and would be run weekly for about two hours, to recharge it. Electricity on the Crisler farm was used for lighting in the barn and the farmhouse and Virginia remembers Jennie having an electric cream separator that she would use daily.

Soon after their marriage Orval and Jennie became proud owners of a wall-mounted telephone that graced their dining room wall. Although telephones in the United States had been around since 1876 when Alexander Graham Bell was granted a patent for his new invention, most households did not have telephones until well after the turn of the twentieth century.[72] In the rural areas they were not common until the decade of the 1910s. Rural telephones that were not on a common battery exchange had a magneto, or hand cranked generator, to produce a high voltage alternating signal to ring the bells of other telephones on the line and to alert the operator.

The telephone operator, usually located several miles away would answer and using her switchboard of up to two hundred phone lines would ring the desired phone number. Typically, telephone operators at that time had to be unmarried between the ages of seventeen and twenty-six, most were female. They were paid only about seven dollars per week for ten to eleven hours per day, six days per week. A female operator who married was forced to leave her job. Operators were the heart of the telephone system and although her main job was to plug callers' phone lines into the phone lines of the people they wanted to speak to, she often acted as the town's information source as well. Operators were often expected to inform customers of election results, storms, train arrivals and much more. [73] Phone customers referred to the early telephone operators as "ringing up central".

After only seven months of marriage Orval's mother, Minnie, became ill and died May 23, 1921 at the age 62. Her death certificate indicates that, like her infant son George William, she also suffered from pernicious anemia. Her obituary which appeared in a local newspaper:

> *"Minnie Delia Crisler, daughter of Anice L. and Jeduthan S. Hopkins, was born near the town of Wyoming in Stark County, Illinois on November 13, 1858, and departed this life at her home near Rensselaer, Indiana, on May 23, 1921.*
>
> *Mrs. Crisler, was one of a family of six children, who came with their parents, to Jasper County, Indiana, in 1864, and the family lived in Jasper and Newton counties until the children were all grown and married.*
>
> *She was united in marriage with William A. Crisler on October 6, 1892 and to this union three children were born,*

two of whom died in infancy. They moved to their present home near Rensselaer in 1910 and on June 13, 1911, Mr. Crisler preceded her into the "Great Beyond."

In 1876 she united with the Methodist Episcopal church at Salem - afterward known as Julian, Indiana, at the time when Mr. Van Scoy had that congregation on his circuit out of Rensselaer, and remained a most faithful member of the church all her life. She was a most active member of the Mt. Ayr church, during her residence in that village, and vicinity, and brought her letter from that church to Rensselaer.

She was always very ambitious, and most devoted to her home and family. One sister, Mrs. Anna Bell, and two brothers, Francis F. and Carey Hopkins, preceded her in death.

Besides her son and daughter, Mr. and Mrs. Orval Crisler, she leaves one sister, Mrs. Etta Robinson of Monon, and one brother, Mr. George Hopkins of Mt. Ayr, of her immediate family, but many other close relatives, who will greatly miss her."

She was laid to rest next to her husband William at Weston Cemetery in Rensselaer.

Pernicious anemia was an untreatable condition prior to 1928. It is a condition caused by the body's inability to absorb Vitamin B12 that results in a myriad of symptoms including fatigue, shortness of breath, heart palpitations, digestive problems, muscle spasms, weakness, as well as tingling and numbness in the extremities. It is especially common in older adults and is most common in individuals of Northern European ancestry. Death was commonly caused by cardiac irregularities that resulted in cardiac arrest.[74]

Almost a year later Orval and Jennie would welcome their first born child, a son, on April 1, 1922. William Orval Crisler was born in Rensselaer Hospital with the assistance of a physician, Dr. Spitler, and was well and healthy for the first few weeks of his life. Young Bill was named William after his paternal grandfather and Orval after his father. The parent's joy was soon dashed, however, when at several weeks of age it was determined that Bill was suffering from a condition called pyloric stenosis which resulted in projectile vomiting each time he was fed. Jennie's attempts at breast feeding were frustrating because she felt she did not have adequate milk production and William was having stomach problems as well. Pyloric stenosis is a condition which results from narrowing of the outlet from the stomach into the pylorus (beginning of the small bowel). In infants, it usually commences between the third and eighth week of life.

Today we know that pyloric stenosis occurs in three out of one-thousand babies in the United States and is four times more likely to occur in firstborn male infants. Pyloric stenosis results in babies who fail to gain weight or actually lose weight. They are often lethargic and less active than usual and they often develop a sunken "soft spot" on their heads, sunken eyes, and a doughy, softened, or wrinkled appearance of the skin on the belly and upper parts of the arms and legs.[75] These can be seen in the photos taken of Bill by his mother Jennie during this time.

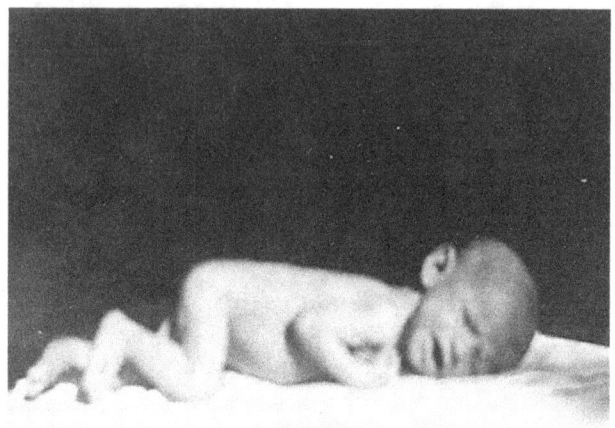

William Orval Crisler. Photo taken by his mother, Jennie,
circa May 1922

Today, a fairly simple surgical procedure can be performed which totally relieves this condition and infants can quickly return to normal health. However, in 1922, this type of surgery was apparently not available. For the young parents it was a long six months of intense care before William outgrew his stenosis. During this time, amateur photographer Jennie took many photographs of her first born, possibly fearing that he might not live and wanting to capture his likeness should the worst happen. Bill, however, did survive those first few months (with his mother's good nursing care) and went on to live a full life of 83 years.

Jennie's nursing classes on infant nutrition/feeding were certainly put to the test during this trying time. During her training at Wesley Hospital ten years previously Jennie had a four week's course in the diet kitchen of the department of Pediatrics which comprised practice in mixing and preparing various foods prescribed for babies that were on the feeding list of the clinic at Northwestern University Medical School. Northwestern was proud to be the first institution in America to establish a laboratory for the modification of cow's milk for infant feeding and to afford nurses and medical students a thorough training in the methods of preparation. [76]

Jennie was busy caring for her first born when she discovered she was pregnant with her second child. Virginia Mae was born March 20, 1923, just a few weeks shy of her brother William's first birthday. Virginia made her appearance at home in the front bedroom on the Rensselaer farm with a physician in attendance. Virginia's birth was followed closely over the next four years by the arrival of three more Crisler children, John Edward, born May 9, 1924, George Hamilton, born July 31, 1925 and Emily Jeannette born September 10, 1927. Imagine, five babies in just over five and a half years! All were born in Rensselaer except for George who was born while the family lived briefly in nearby Rochester, Indiana, about fifty miles from Rensselaer.

Five Crisler children dressed in their Easter finery April 1928

Orval had taken a job there as a manager of a creamery and rented his home farm to another farmer. This soon proved be an unsatisfactory arrangement. According to Orval's daughter, Virginia, Orval was not happy with the way the farmer was managing the land and the farm and he returned to Rensselaer about a year later.

Little did Jennie and Orval know how their family pattern was typical of the time. In 1800 the average number of children born to a white woman was more than seven. By 1900 the figure had fallen to 3.56 children and by 1939 the birthrate had declined by another third. Not only were women having fewer children, they were spacing children closer together and ceasing childbirth at an earlier age. Instead of bearing children into their late thirties, most women stopped giving birth by their early or mid-thirties. Jennie was 36 years old when her youngest child, Emily, was born. As a result of the falling birthrates, fewer years devoted to childbearing, and longer life expectancy in 1900, a typical woman had half her life ahead of her after her last child was born, and at least a decade more than her mother had experienced free of child-rearing responsibilities.[77] In Jennie's case, having completed her child-bearing at age 36, she had another full 58 years of her life ahead of her. In 1920 the average life expectancy for men was just over 56 years and 58 years for women.[78] Both she and Orval would outlive that expectancy.

The other question that begs answering is how couples in the 1920s prevented unwanted pregnancies. We don't know specifically how Orval and Jennie handled this, but we do know that following the birth of Emily there were no more babies. During this time birth control was becoming an issue with women like Margaret Sanger, a New York nurse who devoted her life to educating women about contraception. The birth control movement at that time is thought to have come out of the women's suffrage movement which culminated in August 1920 with the passage of the nineteenth amendment to the constitution and the women's right to vote. In 1916 Margaret Sanger opened the first birth control clinic for women in Brooklyn, New York. During the 1920s couples could use condoms or practice abstinence to prevent unwanted pregnancies. Single-use latex condoms were introduced in the mid 1910s.[79] Hormonal contraception (or birth control pills) would not be available until long after Jennie would have a need for birth control. Birth control pills were not available to women in the United States until the early 1960s.

Those early years for the Crislers must have been hectic and chaotic with five children under the age of six years. But Jennie did have some help at home with a 'hired girl'. Typically 'hired girls' in the 1920s were older female teenagers or single young women who were hired for a few days or weeks to help with household chores or to baby sit.[80] Jennie's hired girl helped her with childcare as well as housecleaning and laundry. Virginia remembers her mother talking about doing laundry when her children were small. Even before breakfast Jennie would have washed the babies' laundry and would have hung up as many as ninety to one hundred cloth diapers in addition to all the other 'little things' to dry each day on the backyard clotheslines. At one point she had three little ones in diapers at the same time.

Jennie had difficulty breast feeding her babies and had to depend on a product called Mellins milk. The popular products of today for infant feeding were not yet invented. In Europe Henri Nestle (of chocolate making fame) had developed an infant formula in the 1860s but it was not available in the United States. Franklin Infant Food, later called Similac, would not be invented until 1923, Enfamil, not until 1959. During the 1920s most mothers relied on dry Mellins milk powder which they would reconstitute with water to feed their infants. An advertisement for Mellins which appeared in an 1896 medical journal states that "fresh cow's milk prepared with Mellin's

Food according to the directions forms a true Liebig's food and is the best substitute for Mother's milk yet produced. Mellins food is not only readily digestible itself but it actually assists to digest milk and other food with which it is mixed."[81]

In addition to maintaining the farm household, feeding her children and husband, tending the garden and her chickens, preserving the food, keeping their laundry and house clean, Jennie made most of the clothing worn by the family. The author remembers Jennie saying that when her children were small her relaxation time was when she was able to sit at her sewing machine in the afternoons while the children napped and she would devote her time to sewing. She used a manual treadle type machine, a hand-operated, single needle machine.

The Rensselaer farm house was small for a family of seven by today's standards. Virginia remembers that although the house had a second story it was not heated so the entire family lived on the first floor year in and year out. On the first floor were four rooms, a living or sitting room, a dining room, a kitchen and one bedroom. There was no bathroom in the house. An outhouse in the back yard was a 'one-holer'. Baths were taken once a week in a galvanized metal tub set up in the kitchen. Water was heated on the wood stove. The eldest child went first followed by the next oldest until all were bathed in the same bath water.

In the bedroom, Jennie and Orval shared a double bed which had a pull-out trundle which provided sleeping for the three little boys—Bill, John and George. Virginia slept in the 'crib' and when baby Emily arrived she slept in a basket in the same bedroom. Central heating was not yet commonly used and the farmhouse was warmed with a wood burner in the living room and the kitchen cook stove. Virginia remembers standing behind the burner in the kitchen on cold winter days to get dressed when it was cold in the bedroom. A large reservoir on the side of the wood stove kept a quantity of water warm for washing dishes, bathing and shaving. Water was carried from the pump at the back yard well on a daily basis to the reservoir in the wood stove.

During the 1920s, much was changing for the American farm family. They would look back on the previous decade as an era of great prosperity. The 1910s, especially the years of World War I (1914–1918) with its military needs and food shortages in Europe, witnessed a booming market for agricultural products in this country. [82] Once the war ended, however, the market for their crops and livestock began to shrink, land values started to decline, and the burden of debt weighed heavily upon many farmers. The last year of any agricultural prosperity was 1920. After 1920 farm income and land values would slide into a twenty-year depression and not emerge from that slump until World War II. Even in the relatively good year of 1920, over a half million of the nation's 6.5 million farms were sold, and others struggled to cope. Midwestern farm bankruptcies would quadruple in 1922 and double again in 1923. Farm households as a percentage of the nation's total fell from 28 to 22 percent over the course of the decade. [83] It is no wonder that Orval made the decision in 1927 to leave agriculture and follow a new career path.

Not only were things changing for the American farm family, but they were changing specifically for the Crisler family. At some point during the first few years of marriage, Orval made a decision that would have a great influence on all the family members. He decided to return to school to get his degree in accounting. He had not been able to complete his last year of high school due to his father's untimely death in 1911. And in the mid 1920s there was no such thing as a GED (General Educational Development), commonly called a General Education Diploma. The GED tests today are a battery of five tests which, when passed, certifies that the taker has high school-level academic skills. These tests would not be developed until World War II. Luckily, Orval was able to enroll in the Chicago-based LaSalle Extension University without having completed his senior year at high school. Located at 4046 Michigan Avenue, LaSalle Extension University offered accounting education (as well as other programs including law and business) via mail order beginning in the 1910s. It was affiliated with the University of Chicago through its adjunct faculty. Eventually LaSalle was found deficient in preparing candidates for careers in professional accounting and state licensing authorities mandated the completion of a bachelor's degree as a prerequisite for sitting for the CPA examination. LaSalle closed its doors to students in 2000 after a ninety year history. [84]

During 1924 Orval would become a Mason when he was initiated March 23, 1924 as an entered apprentice at the Prairie Lodge #125 in Rensselaer, Indiana. Masonic records indicate that he was passed to a Fellowcraft on April 7, 1924 and was raised to Master Mason on April 21, 1924 both at Prairie Lodge. Later in his life, following his move to Chicago, he joined Adelphi Lodge #1029 on September 22, 1943. Adelphi Lodge became Union Park Lodge #610 in 1968 and that is where his Masonic membership remained until his death. [85]

Orval made the risk-taking decision to leave his comfortable existence as a farmer in northwestern Indiana where he had lived his entire life to take a new job in a new occupation in Illinois to support his wife and growing family.

Chapter 4

Crisler Couple—The Middle Years

With his new accounting skills Orval accepted a position as a bookkeeper for Johnson Outboard Motors in Waukegan, Illinois in 1927. The farm in Jasper County, Indiana was sold and the family was ready to move to the city. At that time Waukegan was a growing suburb of Chicago with a population of less than twenty thousand.[86] Johnson Motors was a fairly new firm, established in 1922. Based in Waukegan, Illinois on the Lake Michigan shore, the company would become famous for their brand-name Johnson and Evinrude outboard motors.[87] The family packed themselves into their 1927 Chevrolet coupe for the trip to Waukegan, north of Chicago and about 125 miles northwest of Rensselaer. Virginia remembers Orval hiring a man to drive his family (Jennie and the five children) to Waukegan from Rensselaer. Her memory is that they were "stuffed" into the car for the drive. Year old Emily was in a basket. At an average speed of twenty-five miles per hour it probably took them five hours or more to make the trip.

Once in Waukegan the Crislers lived in a rental home for several months while they waited for their new home on Jackson Street to be completed. Their new home was a bungalow-style house, a form of architecture that probably originated in California in the first decade of the twentieth century. By the 1920s it had spread all over the country. It was very popular with younger members of the middle class as a 'starter house' and was the most popular suburban home during this decade. Many cities, Chicago included, were surrounded by a 'bungalow belt', a ring of suburbs built during the 20s in which the bungalow was the dominant home style. At this time suburbs of the major Midwestern cities, including Chicago, St. Louis and Detroit were experiencing phenomenal growth. In Illinois and Michigan seventy-one new towns were formed during the 1920s. [88]

Cheaper to build and buy than grander homes, bungalow homes were smaller, usually eight to fifteen hundred square feet. Typically, they were one or one-and-one-half story buildings with a pitched roof, wide eaves, and a front porch. The porch was usually supported by massive pillars of stone or brick, enhancing the low profile of the house. Clever interior arrangement of spaces eliminated most of the halls and passages between rooms that characterized more formal Georgian or other European-influenced floor plans of the era. Low ceilings, plain or clear-curved stained oak or pine moldings, and stained or clear-finished wooden floors conveyed a sense of simplicity that had begun to gain adherents as the "mission" and "arts and crafts" furnishing styles. Built-in seats, bureaus, buffets, and tables provided more open space but restricted options in furnishing arrangements.[89]

The Crisler's Waukegan bungalow boasted a one-car detached garage for the family car, typical of most homes built during that time. Because a homeowner didn't add a garage until he purchased his first motor car, the typical garage in many cases was just a converted barn or detached building added after the house was built. Some less-expensive homes were built with detached garages as was the Crisler's. Some more expensive suburban Tudor and colonial-revival type homes began to include the occasional attached garage. [90]

Crisler home in Waukegan, Illinois circa 1935

The Crisler's bungalow on Jackson Street was approximately twelve hundred square feet on one floor with three bedrooms and one bathroom. The three boys shared one bedroom, Virginia and Emily shared the second and their parents had the third bedroom. Electrical power was provided by the Edison Electric Company. Heat was provided by a coal burner in the basement. A coal bin next to the burner stored the coal that was delivered on a regular basis. During the cold winter months Orval had to regularly stoke the coal fire to make sure it didn't go out. At night the fire was 'banked' which means the coal was arranged so that it would burn all night without going out. This, however, often resulted in a cool house in the morning on especially cold winter nights. Without electricity and fans to move air, these early furnaces transported heat by natural convection (warm heated air rising) through ducts from the basement furnace to the rooms above.

The new home had a bathroom complete with a white porcelain flushing toilet, a pedestal sink and a claw foot tub. They no longer had to use the outhouse in the backyard. In 1920 only twenty percent of American homes had a flush toilet, by 1930 the number had risen to fifty percent.[91] It did not, however, have a shower or an on-demand water heater. Before the late 1920s, showers were usually reserved for hospitals, barracks and gymnasiums. When the family wanted to bathe, typically on Saturday evenings, the gas operated hot water heater would be turned on and the hot water would fill the claw-foot tub in the bathroom. There was sufficient water for all five of the Crisler children to bathe, one after the other in the same water, normally the eldest going first.

On weekdays Jennie would have to heat up water in the tea kettle on the kitchen range for Orval to shave each morning. Like most other clean shaven men of the day, Orval used a straight razor to shave his face. Electric shavers were not invented until 1931. A straight razor with open steel blades was the most commonly used razor before the twentieth century. Today they are now chiefly used by barbers. A straight razor consists of a blade sharpened on one edge. The blade can be made of either high-carbon steel, which is slow to hone and strop but dulls more slowly, or stainless steel, which hones and strops quickly and resists rusting, but requires more frequent sharpening.[92] Orval's grandchildren remember Grandpa's straight razor. His strop, used to sharpen the blade, always hung in the bathroom.

In Waukegan, they now had a fully electrified house, although electrical supply was not always dependable and power outages were fairly frequent. In the kitchen Jennie had an ice box that required regular deliveries of ice. The ice man, driving the streets of Waukegan in a horse-drawn wagon similar to the milk man, would make ice deliveries several times each week. Jennie would order her ice by the pound based on her needs. An icebox was the common appliance for providing refrigeration in the home before safe refrigerants made compact mechanical refrigerators useful.

Most iceboxes were made of wood, for ease of construction, insulation, and aesthetics. Many were handsome pieces of furniture. Iceboxes had hollow walls that were lined with tin or zinc and packed with various insulating materials such as cork, sawdust, or straw. The ice box consisted of three parts: the shelves where the food was kept cool, the compartment for the block of ice, and the drip pan underneath. A large block of ice was held in a tray or compartment near the top of the box. Under normal conditions, a one-foot-square block of ice lasted a week, less during warmer weather. Cold air circulated down and around storage compartments in the lower section. Some more expensive models had spigots for draining ice water from a catch pan or holding tank. In less expensive models a drip pan was placed under the box and had to be emptied on a daily basis. In 1923, there were twenty thousand refrigerators in America, and the average cost of a unit was four hundred and fifty dollars.[93] Towards the end of the 1920s, the Crislers would replace their ice box with a monitor-top refrigerator with a motor enclosed in a cylindrical cabinet on top of the refrigerator box. This was a self-contained machine made of steel and porcelain, and the motor was part of the unit, certainly an improvement over its predecessor with its messy, dripping ice box and drip pan.

A Hoosier cabinet graced the kitchen of the new bungalow on Jackson Street as it had the Rensselaer farmhouse kitchen. A Hoosier cabinet (also known simply as a "Hoosier") was a type of kitchen cupboard popular in the first decades of the twentieth century. Named after the Hoosier Manufacturing Company of New Castle, Indiana, they were also made by several other companies, most also located in Indiana. The typical Hoosier cabinet consisted of three parts. The base section usually had one large compartment with a slide-out shelf, and several drawers to one side. Generally it sat on small casters. The top portion was more shallow and had several smaller compartments with doors, with one of the larger lower compartments having a roll-top or tambour. The top and the bottom were joined by a pair of metal channels which served as the guide for a sliding countertop, which usually had a pair of shallow drawers affixed to its underside. One particularly distinctive item was the combination flour-bin/sifter, a tin hopper that could be used without having to remove it from the cabinet.[94]

Even though the family had moved to the suburbs, Jennie continued her small backyard vegetable garden. She continued to 'put up' her garden products including her Chili Sauce which her daughter Emily still makes today. A lot of Jennie's time was still taken up in preparing and cooking meals for her family. Data from 1920 reveals that for the American housewife an average forty-four hours were spent on preparing meals and cleaning up after them each week. As vitamins began to be discovered starting in 1912 consumers became much more cognizant of the nutritional importance of items including fruit, vegetables and milk.

One of the most striking developments of the 1920s was the shift toward processed foods. Where previously housewives had prepared food from scratch at home (peeling potatoes, shelling peas, plucking chickens, or grinding coffee beans), an increasing number of Americans purchased foods that were ready-to-cook. World War I had brought about new methods of canned and frozen foods. The new kitchen appliances including gas stoves, electric refrigerators, and other labor-saving kitchen devices enabled easy preparation and storage of food and beverages. New foods introduced during the 1920s included Wonder Bread (1920), Popsicles (1924), Peter Pan Peanut Butter (1928) and Velveeta Cheese (1928). By 1927 *Woman's Home Companion* magazine had advertisements for the following products we now take for granted including Campbell's Vegetable Beef Soup, Maxwell House Coffee, Flesichmann Yeast, Aunt Jemima Pancake Flour, Brer Rabbit Molasses, Borden Eagle Brand Condensed Milk and Minute Tapioca. Another 1920s invention was frozen food. In 1922 Charles Birdseye formed his own company and by 1930 was selling twenty-six different frozen vegetables, fruits, fish and meats. Following January 1920, when Prohibition went into effect, Americans sought a variety of other beverages choices. While alcohol consumption went underground, there was an increase in the cocoa and chocolate consumption, as well as soft drinks, coffee and tea. [95]

Laundry chores for the family of seven continued to be a time consuming endeavor. For Jennie this chore became a little easier when Orval fashioned a laundry machine from an old washing barrel to which he hooked a small electric motor. Following agitation in the soapy hot water, clothes were pulled through a manual wringer perched on top of the washing barrel. From there, the clean clothes were sent to one of two sinks for rinsing, the first sink had plain cold water, and the second sink contained cold water with bluing. Bluing was commonly used in the 1920s to improve the appearance of textile fabrics. White fabrics have a tendency to acquire a slight color cast after use (usually gray or yellow) because they can never be cleaned perfectly.[96] Adding a trace of blue color to the slightly off-white color of these fabrics made them appear whiter. Bleach could further enhance the preferred white appearance. Clothes were then toted to the back yard in laundry baskets to be hung outside on the clothes lines or in inclement weather they were hung up to dry in the basement. Hanging outside was preferable because the sun further improved the whitening qualities of bleach and bluing. Underclothing was not ironed in the Crisler household (although it was in some), but the rest of the clothes worn by the family, in addition to most of the table linens and bed sheets were ironed. Monday comprised a full day of washing for Jennie;

Tuesday was usually devoted to ironing, sometimes starching certain pieces such as Orval's dress shirts for work. Any item of clothing that needed to be repaired waited until ironing day for mending. Before clothes could be ironed, those that were starched had to be sprinkled with water or dampened and rolled up for an hour or two so that they would iron smoothly. Jennie probably got her first electric iron when the family moved to Waukegan where they had a more dependable electrical supply.

In Waukegan, the Crisler children would all begin their elementary school education. The grammar (elementary) school, named the West School, was a short two and a half blocks away from the Crisler's Jackson Street home, close enough to walk to school and home again at noon-time for lunch. Following completion of eighth grade the Crislers would all graduate and go on to the high school. Waukegan Township High School, located about two blocks away, provided classes for ninth through twelve grades.

During the children's first few years of life, including their years of elementary school Jennie made most of their clothing. At the beginning of each school year she would purchase a bolt of blue poplin shirt fabric for the boys and make each of them three new shirts. The boys would wear knickers (short for knickerbockers) made from corduroy or wool. Knickers were short knee-length pants worn by boys less than age fourteen in the 1920s and early 1930s. They were worn with long socks that would be tucked under the band of the knickers. Similarly, she made dresses for the girls and even 'bloomers' for underneath their school dresses. Virginia remembers getting her first store-bought dress when she was in third grade at a cost of forty-nine cents.

Elementary education was changing at this time. By 1918 all states had passed laws requiring children to attend at least elementary school. Teachers were becoming better educated themselves. At least a two-year course at a state teachers' college or normal school became standard for minimum teaching requirement, and especially at the high school level, a four-year college degree became commonplace. Salaries, never high in the predominately female profession, did nevertheless improve considerably from an average of $871 in 1920 to $1,441 by 1940.

For students, the typical school day included a combination of study periods for reading textbooks, writing and solving math problems and recitation periods. During recitation sessions students told their teacher what the book had said or how the problem should be worked out. Teachers wanting to show graphics of a particular topic would often use the stereopticon. Virginia remembers the teacher passing a hand-held stereopticon around the classroom so that each student could view the illustrative slide. Textbooks became more colorful and attractive, more up-to-date, and more often supplemented by flash cards, workbooks, and filmstrips in schools that could afford them.

Larger urban schools were able to offer a broader choice of courses, particularly at the high school level, including mechanical arts, home economics, typing, as well as physical education, art and music.[97]

Home entertainment for the Crislers was provided by the new medium—the radio. We know that the Crislers had their own radio by the time the 1930 census was taken.[98] Following World War I numerous radio stations started up and by the early 1920s a 'radio music box' could be purchased for fifty to one hundred dollars. Chicago's early AM radio station WMAQ came into existence in 1922. As more radios were purchased and more radio stations started, radio programming improved. It grew into a kind of family centerpiece when the parents and children would gather around the radio after dinner to listen to static-y news, music, and entertainment. The National Broadcasting Corporation (NBC) was formed in 1926, Columbia Broadcasting System (CBS) a year later. The American Broadcasting Company (ABC) would not make its appearance until the 1940s. One of the most popular early radio programs was the 'Amos 'n' Andy' show which debuted in Chicago on WMAQ in March 1928. Across the country many radio listeners scheduled their agendas around the program's fifteen-minute, five-night-per-week, seven o'clock broadcast. Even President Calvin Coolidge demanded to be undisturbed when 'Amos 'n' Andy' was on. The show was sponsored by Pepsodent (a popular brand of tooth paste) from 1929–1937 and by Campbell's Soup from 1937–1943. Waukegan's own home-town boy, Jack Benny, made his debut on the Ed Sullivan radio show in early 1931.[99] Virginia remembers listening to numerous radio shows while growing up in Waukegan, including Jack Armstrong, Smiling Jack, Little Orphan Annie, Gildersleeve, Amateur Hour, Edgar Bergen and Charlie McCarthy, The Shadow and Fibber Magee and Molly.

Children's health is always an issue for young parents, no less for Jennie and Orval and their young children in the late 1920s. Their eldest son Bill had beat the odds and survived his first few months while suffering from a life threatening medical condition. Other health concerns, however, were still lurking and possible. Prior to the advent of the development of antibiotics for common bacterial infections and prior to the development of life protecting childhood immunizations children were at risk for numerous serious and possibly even fatal medical conditions. Without the benefit of antibiotics, a sore throat caused by streptococcus (strep throat) could end up in rheumatic fever and life threatening heart murmurs. Luckily, aspirin for fever reduction was available following its approval for sale without a physician's prescription in 1915. Most children during their first decade of life were victims of a variety of childhood illnesses including chicken pox, measles, German measles, and mumps. Most were not life threatening but some were not without the possibility of devastating side effects and even the rare possibility of death. During this period some children suffered from meningitis, diphtheria, tetanus, whooping cough and others. Today children are protected from all of these illnesses and several others through early childhood immunizations. The Crisler children had their share of childhood illnesses including measles, mumps and chicken pox but, luckily, without any serious complications.

The family had just been settled into their new home on Jackson Street in Waukegan for a year or so when in October 1929 the stock market crash would set off changes that would have significant repercussions for the Crislers as well as the rest of the country. The Great Depression would last throughout the decade of the 1930s, impacting every aspect of life in the United States as well as around the world. Only the massive economic demands of World War II would bring an end to the Great Depression. Virginia remembers her parents having conversations about the possibility of losing their new house (which according to the 1930 census was worth nine thousand dollars). When Orval and Jennie had made the decision to put the proceeds from the sale of the Rensselaer farm into their new home in Waukegan versus putting a portion of that into savings, they opted to put a portion of it into savings. Sadly, with the collapse of banking, all of their savings were lost. The Crisler children would also lose their savings, in most cases just a few dollars, but a fortune to a small child.

Luckily for the family, Orval was able to continue working throughout the depression years unlike many others across the country who lost their jobs. By April 1930, four million Americans were out of work. By the end of 1931 that number had grown to 13.5 million. The Great Depression was particularly severe in Chicago and the surrounding area (including Waukegan) because of the city's reliance on manufacturing, the hardest hit sector nationally. Only fifty percent of the Chicagoans who had worked in the manufacturing sector in 1927 were still working there in 1933.[100] By 1932, the worst year, 750,000 Chicagoans were out of work and only 800,000 had jobs. Over 160,000 families received relief from private and local agencies.[101] We don't know for sure how the depression affected Orval's income, but in 1929 the average per capita income was $629 and in 1932 it was $425. Many employers, rather than dismiss workers with experience and skills, would try to keep them at reduced hours and wages.

At some point during the early 1930s Orval's job at Johnson Outboard was affected and he did lose his job. Luckily he was appointed by Illinois Governor Horner to the very important position of Accounting Supervisor for Lake County, Illinois (where Waukegan is located) for the Illinois Emergency Relief Commission. He worked there one year when he received an offer from Paul Pettingill & Company for a position on their staff as a junior accountant. Within a few months he was advanced to Senior Accountant. His job often entailed business travel to southern Indiana, to Crawfordsville, a four hundred mile round trip from Waukegan. Virginia remembers that during the Depression her parents had a twenty-five dollar per month mortgage payment and her mother had a budget of five dollars per week for groceries for their family of seven.

In the Crisler household, one of the most obvious effects of the Depression could be seen in the family's dietary options. They were fortunate that they did not lose their home and Orval was able to stay employed, but there were negative changes that affected their lives on a daily basis. Virginia can remember many meatless meals. Lunchtime on school days was often canned pork and beans with bread and butter or rice pudding with raisins and sugar (if it was available) and milk. Like many other middle class families throughout the country, the Crislers depended on their home garden with their home canned produce, ate less meat and more beans, pancakes, and macaroni and cheese. Americans went back to making their own clothing (although Jennie never really had changed this habit) and doing their own home repairs.

But as challenging as times were for the Crislers, many others were finding life during the Depression years much more difficult. Some were doing without food; some were without homes and living as homeless people. It was not uncommon for Jennie to have a knock at her back door and a homeless person requesting a meal. She never turned them away and shared what she could with the less fortunate. Using the telephone for local or long-distance calls came to be regarded as an unaffordable luxury for many Americans. The number of telephones in service declined from over 20 million in 1930 to fewer than 17 million by 1933. As many as one-sixth of families doubled up and shared living quarters. Children increasingly took small jobs running errands, mowing lawns, shoveling snow, baby-sitting, or delivering newspapers to supplement the family income. Virginia remembers that her three brothers had paper routes and sold magazines door-to-door to their neighbors. Virginia earned fifteen cents per hour baby-sitting for her neighbor's children. Throughout the country 'making do' with hand-me-down clothes, day-old bakery bread, shoes repaired with cardboard, and coats relined with old blankets became common for many Americans.[102]

Although the 1930s were a trying time for the Crisler family, as it was for many others all over the world, they also enjoyed some good times. 1933 brought the Chicago World's Fair to the Lake Michigan shoreline and Orval took his entire family to experience 'A Century of Progress' as it was titled. Planned to coincide with the city's centennial, the theme of the fair was technological innovation. Its motto was 'Science Finds, Industry Applies, Man Conforms' and its architectural symbol was the Sky Ride, a transporter bridge perpendicular to the shore on which one could ride from one end of the fair to the other.[103] The 1933 Chicago Fair was so successful that it was continued in 1934 and the Crislers attended both years. Virginia remembers riding a brand-new invention, the escalator, which fascinated her. She also remembers Greyhound buses that provided transportation on the fair site covering a three mile stretch of lakefront real estate. Orval spent $2.25 each day for the entire family to visit the fair, fifty cents for both he and Jennie and twenty-five cents each for the five children.

At home, in addition to radio programming, simple board games as well as checkers and the card game Rummy provided entertainment for the Crislers. The board game Monopoly, following its release in 1935, became a family favorite. Toys were fairly simple. As a small child, Virginia remembers playing with oatmeal boxes that she and her siblings used to resemble make-believe 'butter churns', similar to the ones they had seen when their father had worked for the creamery in Rochester, Indiana. Later, as teenagers the five Crisler children attended Epworth League meetings at nearby Waukegan Methodist Church. Following church services Sunday dinner was enjoyed in the early afternoon. Emily and Virginia were responsible for making a cake for dessert on Saturday afternoon in preparation for Sunday dinner. Then at supper time on Sunday evening the family started a routine which Orval and Jennie would continue for the rest of their lives. Rather than eating a supper meal, they would enjoy fresh popped corn with melted butter along with a soft drink, usually coca cola, or a "brown cow", a float of root beer over vanilla ice cream.

Holidays were celebrated quite simply during the Depression years. Virginia remembers dyeing hard-boiled eggs on the Saturday before Easter and getting a basket of candy on Easter morning. Fourth of July was celebrated with a parade in town and fireworks at home. Christmas was a simple holiday with just a few toys for each child and always a stocking with a fresh orange and 'penny candy' or one candy cane. Rather than trick-or-treating door to door in Waukegan, Orval and Jennie had a party for their children to celebrate Halloween in their own basement. Jennie was afraid that her neighbors would accuse the Crisler boys of doing mischievous pranks and if they were at home she knew they could not be falsely accused. Activities like 'bobbing for apples' with popcorn and apple cider and other treats were enjoyed by all the Crisler children and their friends. Birthdays were celebrated with a birthday cake at home with the family and simple gifts.

Vacations were infrequent for the Crislers during the trying time of the Depression, in fact for most of their growing-up years. Visits to family members and some of Jennie's nursing school classmates were the extent of their vacation trips.

The Social Security Act was signed into law on August 14, 1935 by President Franklin D. Roosevelt. In addition to several provisions for the general welfare, the new act created a social insurance program designed to pay retired workers age 65 or older a continuing income. Workers and employers were required to register for the new benefit by January 1, 1937 when workers would begin acquiring credits toward old-age insurance benefits and payroll taxes would start to be collected.[104] Orval explained the new Social Security law to his children, telling them that they would benefit from this new legislation but that he probably would not. In actuality, Orval would benefit from social security and would receive more than twenty years of social security benefits following his retirement at age 72 in 1965.

The Crisler children planned to graduate from Waukegan's West School at the completion of eighth grade and go on to attend the Waukegan Township High School just a short walk from their home. But prior to any of them completing their high school education, Orval made a job move which took the family from Waukegan to Chicago. Orval was offered a job opportunity as an accountant with the Gulbransen Piano Company in 1938 and the family moved to the Austin area on the far west side of Chicago. All of the children had to transfer from Waukegan schools to the Chicago school system. The oldest four including Bill, Virginia, John and George, would attend Austin High School in 1938. Youngest Emily would transfer to Hayes Elementary School. For the eldest, Bill and Virginia, this meant a school transfer just as they were both entering their senior year of high school. For just over a year the family lived in a rented home at 1447 North Austin Boulevard within the Austin High School district. In early 1939 they would move to their new house at 5930 Race Avenue, a spacious home of approximately two thousand square feet, significantly larger than their bungalow house in Waukegan. The three story frame house featured a wide front porch, a small front and back yard, four bedrooms on the second floor and two finished but unheated rooms on the third floor, a one car detached garage and a full basement which housed the coal-burning furnace, coal bin, and a water heater.

Crisler home on Race Avenue, Chicago circa 1940

As the 1930s were coming to a close the Crisler family finances were looking up. Orval had a new, better paying job as an accountant with the Gulbransen Piano Company and the family had a new, larger home. Their oldest children, Bill and Virginia, would graduate from Austin High School in January, 1941, the class of 40½. Austin High School had an enrollment of close to eight thousand students during the 1930s, making it the largest co-educational high school in the world. It was so large and crowded for a few years in the late 1930s that students were in two buildings including a branch at Hayes Grammar School. For a while classes were held on double shifts. Bill and Virginia were in the last mid-term class to graduate in January. Subsequent classes would resume a more usual June graduation schedule.

Following high school graduation, Virginia would go off to comptometer (early mechanical adding machine) school with classes in the Chicago Merchandise Mart in downtown Chicago and later take college courses at the Chicago campus of Northwestern University (based in Evanston, Illinois). Bill would take a job performing electrical drafting in Chicago. John and George attended Austin High and did not graduate before they enlisted in the U.S. Navy and left to serve their country during World War II. Emily transferred to Hayes Elementary School and later went on to graduate from Austin High.

Meanwhile, Jennie maintained the home front as a full-time homemaker. She never learned to drive a car so had to depend on getting around 'on shank's mare' (as she would say), on foot or using public transportation, even for her groceries. When her boys were young she would walk to the local A & P (Atlantic and Pacific) grocery store and have one of her boys bring along their little red wagon so they could help her by carting the groceries home. Orval would drive the family car, a 1937 Chevrolet, to work and the children would walk to school. Public transportation in the city was available for longer trips. Jennie's world centered around her home and she continued to keep house, raising some of her produce in her small backyard garden, baking and preparing family meals. She would also sew for her family, although more and more often store-bought clothing was purchased. Jennie was an accomplished seamstress and needle-woman. She enjoyed crocheting, knitting and tatting and used these skills to provide clothing for her family as well as provide items to beautify her home.

Even though things were looking up for the Crisler family in Chicago, the political environment in Europe and around the world was disintegrating. In 1939, with the German invasion of Poland and the outbreak of what would become World War II, the Crislers as well as their fellow Americans were anxious about the future. On December 7, 1941 when Pearl Harbor was bombed and the United States entered the war effort, the Crislers had three military-eligible sons. Eldest son Bill graduated from high school in January 1941 and after the war broke out he would try to enlist but was medically deferred. Sons John and George would enlist in the U.S. Navy. John would serve on the 'USS Bunker Hill', an aircraft carrier in the Pacific Theatre of Operation as an aerial photographer. John would meet his future wife, June Wilson, while at Fort Sill, Oklahoma where he was stationed while training for his photography job with the Navy. John and June married in December 1943. George also met his future wife while stationed in Oklahoma during naval training. He and Barbara Dee Bell married in 1944 in Durant, Oklahoma.

Once the United States entered the war in late 1941 following the bombing of Pearl Harbor on December 7, 1941, there were many changes on the home front which would affect the Crisler family on a personal level. One of the major sacrifices that was required of most people on the home front was involuntary and unprecedented rationing of some twenty essential items by the federal government. The first was sugar rationing which went into effect in the spring of 1942 and did not end until August 1945 with sugar rationing lasting in some parts of the country until 1947. Purchases of sugar were limited to twelve ounces per individual per week.

Each member of the family was issued ration books by the Office of Price Administration (OPA). These books contained stamps and gave precise details of the amounts of certain types of food that citizens were allowed. Rationing insured that each person could get their fair share of the items that were in short supply due to the war effort and import reductions. In addition to sugar, other rationed items included meat, butter, eggs, milk, chocolate, coffee, and cooking oil. When families could not get butter, they resorted to oleomargarine (margarine) that came in a package as a white product. A small enclosed red button or packet of yellow food coloring would be squeezed into the margarine and kneaded until the color was evenly distributed and streak-free. Non-food items that were rationed included gasoline, oil and grease, as well as kerosene, automobile tires, shoes, and household appliances. Scarcity of these items stemmed from a variety of reasons. Canned foods were rationed because tin went into armaments and cans for soldiers' C rations, coffee, because the ships that would ordinarily carry the coffee beans from South America had been diverted for military purposes, and shoes, because the Army alone needed some fifteen million pairs of combat boots. [105]

Initially, in order to get the required ration stamps, Jennie would have gone to her local elementary school (probably Hayes School where daughter Emily attended elementary school) where teachers and other volunteers took depositions as to how much sugar she already had at home and then issued ration books containing coupons good for a fifty-two-week supply.

Different colored ration stamps denoted various essentials—red stamps for meat, butter and fats, blue stamps for canned foods such as peas and beans. Meat rationing was complicated by the fact that each cut required a different number of red stamps. On average, each person was allowed two pounds of meat each week.

Rationed gasoline had an even more elaborate system. Each motorist was assigned a windshield sticker with the appropriate letter of priority, from 'A' to 'E'. If the car was driven for pleasure, the driver was given an 'A' stamp, good for three to five gallons of gas per week. 'B' stickers were for commuters whose gas allotment was determined by their distance from work. The highest priority sticker, the 'E' sticker was given to policemen, clergymen and occasionally politicians. Orval would have been given a 'B' stamp since he commuted to work to his job at Gulbransen Piano, about a six mile trip one way.[106]

Rationing was for items that were in short supply. There were shortages for other items that just were not available at any cost. For example, Jennie, Emily and Virginia could not purchase silk stockings because silk was diverted for the manufacture of parachutes. Nylon had not yet been invented. They, like other American women, went bare legged. Some inventive women created the illusion of a seam down the back of the leg by applying a stripe with an eyebrow pencil. (Note: seamless stockings would not become commonplace until the 1950s, pantyhose not until the late 1960s).

The Crislers, like the rest of their neighbors, were encouraged to conserve food, salvage essential materials and buy War Bonds regularly. The family was diligent in salvaging tin foil which would bring fifty cents for a hefty size ball, scrap paper, tin cans, and even bacon grease (used in the manufacture of ammunitions). Americans were so successful in their salvaging efforts that by the end of the war scrap was supplying much of the steel and half of the tin needed for American weapons production.

Jennie continued her small backyard garden while others who had not gardened in many years took up gardening under the Victory Garden program. Soon after Pearl Harbor, the U.S. Secretary of Agriculture came up with the idea of 'victory gardens'. Not only were there shortages of certain food items, but the labor and transportation shortages made it difficult to harvest and move fruits and vegetables to market. In 1943 Americans planted 20.5 million 'victory gardens' and the harvest accounted for at least one third of all vegetables consumed in the country that year. Housewives were encouraged to can their own vegetables and contribute to another of the government's aims for the home front—the creation of a healthy citizenry.[107]

When the U. S. government needed monies to finance the war, War Bonds were developed that could be purchased in denominations ranging from $25.00 to $10,000. Americans were encouraged to use ten percent of their money to purchase $25.00 Series E bonds at a cost of $18.75. When held to maturity in ten years the bond would be worth its face value of $25.00.[108]

Another unexpected outcome of the war was the increase in the number of marriages. During the 1930s while the country was still in the throes of the Depression, many young adults postponed marriage or did not marry at all. The war changed everything. The deprivation of the 30s was followed by war time indulgence and anticipation of an even better life when the war was over. The marriage rate increased greatly in 1942. Some couples married quickly before the husband shipped out.

In the Crisler family, eldest daughter, Virginia, would be the first to marry in August 1943, followed shortly by younger brother John in December 1943 and in 1944 by younger brother George.

Wedding Photo of Virginia and Leslie Simpson August 1943

Wedding photo of John and June Crisler December 1943

Wedding photo of George and Barbara Crisler 1944

Virginia's new husband, Leslie (nicknamed Les) Simpson, would go off to service in the U. S. Navy just weeks after their marriage.

While Les was off to war, Virginia did her part towards the war effort by taking a job at the Chicago Buick plant (located in suburban Melrose Park). During the war years no automobiles were manufactured and existing auto manufacturing facilities were converted to support the war effort. Virginia applied for a job as a comptometer operator but was offered a job as an airplane engine test engineer because of her math background. Virginia and her co-workers sat behind a concrete wall with two sheets of bullet proof glass between them and the Pratt and Whitney airplane engines that they were testing. The test engineers put the engines through the same cycles and stresses that they would undergo while in flight. They took readings of the dials and computed fuel and air ratios using a slide rule (no calculators).

Diversion of men from the labor pool into the military, as well as the increased production needed to support the war effort, prompted the federal government to undertake a nationwide campaign to recruit women into the work force. "Rosie the Riveter" became the symbol for women workers in the American defense industries. Between 1940 to 1945 the number of female workers rose by fifty percent, from twelve to eighteen million. Little did Virginia or her family know at that time what a significant social change this was, changing the relationship between women and the workplace. As a result, during the war years employment outside the home for women became socially acceptable and even desirable, forever changing how Americans viewed women in the workforce.[109]

Life would slowly return to normalcy after 1945 when World War II came to an end. May 1945 marked V-E Day (Victory in Europe) and August 1945 marked V-J Day (Victory over Japan) with the surrender of the Japanese ending the war in the Pacific. Sons John and George would come home from their war-time duties and return to civilian life. Son-in-law Les Simpson had been discharged in March 1944 following a service related injury. However, in late 1945, returning soldiers and sailors were faced with a severe shortage of housing. A byproduct both of the depression years of the 1930s, when little housing had been constructed and the 1941-1945 war years, when housing construction stopped entirely, a severe housing shortage faced World War II veterans and their families. The shortages grew steadily worse until about 1948, when a massive housing boom finally caught up with demand. This worst housing shortage in United States history would impact the Crisler children as well. Sons John and George would return with their brides to the Chicago home of their parents following the war. Virginia and Les lived for a short time with his parents, James and Jeanie Simpson, and then were lucky to find a small basement apartment in Chicago not far from their parents.

In the immediate post war years, with three of their five children married, Jennie and Orval became grandparents. Daughter Virginia was the first to bless them with a grandchild when grandson James Russell Simpson was born in March 1945. James was soon followed by a granddaughter, Doris Jean Crisler in July, 1945, born to John and his wife, June. Then in July, 1946, George and Barbara blessed them with another grandson, Larry George Crisler.

Crisler Family at Christmas 1949 Back row (l to r): Bill, Jennie, Orval, Barbara, George, June, John Front row: Dorothy, Emily, Larry, Doris Jean, Virginia, Jim. On floor, Leslie Ann

These grandchildren joined many others throughout the country as part of the dramatic post-World War II baby boom. The term 'baby boomer' has come to denote a person born between 1946 and 1964, reflecting the increase in birth rate following World War II. In the United States approximately 79 million babies were born during the Baby Boom years.[110]

In 1948, eldest son Bill married Dorothy Olson and their first child, Peter William, was born in March 1949 followed by Shirley Joy in 1950, Charles Timothy (Tim) in 1955, Karin Sue in 1959 and Carol Louise in 1961.

Wedding photo of Bill and Dorothy April 1948

Bill and Dorothy and their growing family lived in the Chicago area but would move to the Louisville, Kentucky area in the mid 1950s for Bill's job with the General Electric Company. George and Barbara would move to Dallas, Texas with their son Larry. Another son, Gary Scott Crisler, was born in 1959.

Chapter 5

Crisler Couple–The Later Years

The 1950s would bring many changes to the Crisler family as their family continued to grow with additional grandchildren. Orval was working his way up the company ladder at Gulbransen Piano Company with increased financial responsibilities as comptroller, then secretary/treasurer. Jennie continued to fulfill her role as homemaker like many other wives of that era. In the house on Race Avenue, John and June and their children continued to live with Orval and Jennie in an upstairs apartment. John's family grew with the addition of Edith Lynn in 1949, John Hamilton (known by Bud in the family, not to be confused with his father John) in 1953. Helen Ann joined the family in 1960 after the family's move to Glen Ellyn. Son John also worked for Gulbransen Piano Company in the piano action regulating department. Daughter Virginia and her husband, Les Simpson, provided additional grandchildren with the birth of Leslie Ann in 1947, Paul Alan in 1951 and Lauran Elizabeth in 1956.

Youngest daughter, Emily, lived at home with her parents while working for a Chicago bank as a bank teller. She married Lyle William Seefeldt on June 14, 1953 in a church ceremony at the family's church, Austin Methodist Church, not far from their Race Avenue home.

Emily and Lyle's only child, a daughter, Cathleen Ellen Seefeldt, was born in September 1960.

Wedding photo of Emily and Lyle Seefeldt June 1953

Unlike their mother (and mother-in-law), Jennie's daughters and daughters-in-law all delivered their babies in a hospital under a physician's care preceded by months of pre-natal office visits. By 1950 less than twelve percent of births were occurring in the home.[111] While all of Jennie's children (except for the first) were born at home with a physician in attendance, her grandchildren were all born in the hospital, reflecting the perception that childbirth as a natural life cycle event had shifted. In the new, medically dominated culture, pregnancy was now perceived more as an illness, and a pregnant woman, or woman in labor perceived as a patient.[112]

In 1952, following their youngest daughter Emily's wedding to Lyle Seefeldt, Orval and Jennie would leave the city and move to the Chicago suburbs. They purchased a home in the village of Glen Ellyn, about twenty miles from their home on Race Avenue. Glen Ellyn was considered to be an affluent suburban community.

In the mid 1950s, there were approximately 15,500 inhabitants of the village that was served by a suburban commuter railroad, the Northwestern Railroad, to downtown Chicago.[113] John and June and their children moved with them to Glen Ellyn. The Crisler's move to the suburbs mirrored what was happening around the country as the post war economy resulted in growth and expansion to meet the housing and consumer demands. Massive suburban expansion helped to meet the housing needs of the returning veterans and their growing families.

Crisler home in Glen Ellyn circa 1955

At the time their move to Glen Ellyn, all of Orval and Jennie's children were married and making lives of their own. Oldest son Bill and his growing family were living in the Chicago suburb of Des Plaines, Illinois, not far from the soon to be developed O'Hare Airport. Bill was working as an electrical draftsman while wife Dorothy was a stay-at-home mom with children Peter, Shirley, and Timothy. Virginia and her family, including husband Les and children, Jim, Leslie and Paul, were living in close-by suburban Wheaton, about two miles from the Crisler's home in Glen Ellyn. George, Barbara and their son, Larry Crisler, were living in Dallas, Texas. Youngest daughter Emily and her husband were living in the growing Chicago suburban community of South Holland, Illinois, about forty miles southeast of the city.

Jennie's daughters, Virginia and Emily, along with her daughters-in-law, Dorothy, June and Barbara, all lived far different lives than Jennie had before them. Many technological advances had made keeping house far easier than that experienced by Jennie when she was having and raising her family in the 1920s and 1930s. Housekeeping and child rearing were considered ideal female roles during the 1950s, and the expectations were high for young women during this time. Following World War II, when women had joined the workforce as 'Rosie the Riveter', women were once again expected to

73

resume their roles as housewives and mothers and give up their jobs to returning servicemen. The perfect 50s mother was now supposed to stay home and nurture her children and husband.

For Jennie, though, life in the suburbs was not too different than it had been on Race Avenue. Thankfully, their new house no longer relied on a coal furnace, but featured an oil fueled furnace in the basement that provided central heating for the entire house. Residential air conditioning was not available yet. The small kitchen had the latest appliances including refrigerator and gas stove, but no dishwasher. The basement laundry area contained an electric washing machine but no dryer. In addition to an electric iron, Jennie had a mangle iron which she used to press her bed sheets and other flat linens. She continued to hang her laundry on the clotheslines in the back yard.

Orval had a slightly longer commute to work, but the advantages of suburban living made it worthwhile. Jennie continued to depend on Orval, her son, John, or daughter-in-law June, to drive her since she had not learned to drive an automobile. She would often walk to downtown Glen Ellyn, a comparatively short mile-long walk away, and there she could visit the post office, make small purchases and attend church at Glen Ellyn Methodist Church. A commuter train line provided service from Glen Ellyn to downtown Chicago. She would walk to the train station and use the train to go downtown to the Chicago 'loop' for more major shopping at well known Chicago department stores like Carson, Pirie, and Scott and Marshall Fields. She enjoyed keeping house, caring for her grandchildren, gardening in her small suburban yard which included flowers, vegetables and fruit trees in the small side yard on Greenfield Avenue. She continued her thrifty ways of canning and preserving certain foods as she had always done. She found a small patch of wild mint in a vacant lot not far from her house and used it to make fresh mint jelly. Son-in-law Les appreciated her mint jelly for a favorite dish, roast leg of lamb. Fruit trees provided cherries for pies and preserves. Home grown tomatoes, onions and green peppers were the basis for her home-made chili sauce. Her apple trees made delicious home-made applesauce and apple pies.

With the growing number of grandchildren, she continued to enjoy her hand crafts and at Christmas each grandchild, sixteen in all, could count on a hand-made gift from Grandma Crisler. I fondly remember a felt skirt she made for me in the mid 1950s when the 'Poodle Skirt' was popular. The 'poodle skirt' was a full, swing skirt, made of felt material, gathered at the waist and worn with crinolines underneath it and decorated with a poodle dog. Mine was chocolate brown, tan and teal blue and I loved it. I remember wearing it to school in the third grade and getting compliments from the teachers and how proud I was that my grandmother had made it for me. I think it was the first time that I really appreciated my 'home-made' clothing. It was obviously a far better quality product than anything available on the market at the time. In the 1960s, she made 'crazy quilts' for many of her grandchildren. These were crafted from scraps of corduroy that she pieced together, then embellished by hand with embroidered 'feather' stitching and completed by hand-tying the layers together.

As they entered their later years of life, Orval and Jennie were involved with their children and grandchildren but more so with John's children, Jean, Edith, John (Bud) and Helen, since they lived with them. They made efforts to visit with all of their children and grandchildren on a regular basis. Bill and his family would move to the Louisville, Kentucky area in the mid 1950s. Their family would grow with the addition of Karin, born in 1959 and Carol, born in 1961. About the same time, Virginia and her family would move east to the Philadelphia, Pennsylvania area and Lauran would join the family in 1956. George and his family continued to live in the Dallas, Texas area. Their youngest child, Gary, was born in 1959. Only son John and daughter Emily and their families would remain in the immediate Chicago area. In the late 1950s and early 1960s, Orval's job with Gulbransen involved annual road trips when he would visit various Gulbransen dealers around the country. I can remember photos of their trips and postcards from the western and southwestern states, including Carlsbad Caverns and Texas. I also remember a photograph taken by Orval of Jennie amidst a beautiful field of Texas bluebells.

Church played an integral part of Orval and Jennie's life and they were lifelong members of the Methodist church, from Rensselaer, to Waukegan, to Austin, to Glen Ellyn and later in life to Dunedin, Florida. Orval applied his accounting skills while serving as a treasurer at his church, both in Glen Ellyn and Dunedin. They both were members of Masonic organizations, Orval in the Masons and Jennie in the Order of Eastern Star.

In 1963 at the age of 72, Jennie was diagnosed with breast cancer which required dramatic surgery (radical mastectomy) followed by a round of radiation therapy. Luckily, she had a lot of family support with her son John and wife June close-by to help with trips to the doctor's office and hospital. She also had a positive outlook and was successful in battling her cancer diagnosis and never had a reoccurrence.

The time for retirement was fast approaching. Orval worked until he was 72 years old before he retired and at that point made the significant decision to move to a warmer climate. In November 1966 Orval and Jennie moved to Dunedin on the west coast of Florida, just north of St. Petersburg. There they purchased a small ranch-style home with two bedrooms, one bath, a garage for their one auto, and a Florida room where they watched television and could view their back yard and garden area. A small back yard with several citrus trees kept former farmer Orval happy. Jennie enjoyed the citrus that came out of their backyard and enjoyed freezing her own orange juice.

Orval and Jennie outside their home in Dunedin,
Florida circa 1975

While in Florida, Orval and Jennie quickly adapted to the new lifestyle of retirees and enjoyed the more temperate climate of central Florida. They did not miss the cold Chicago winters at all. Jennie took up new crafts and learned to make baskets with pine needles and raffia and continued her other handcrafts, making gifts for family and friends. One year Orval used his wood working skills to make wooden wastebaskets for his grandchildren as Christmas gifts.

Visits from family were more and more important to them as the couple grew older and long road trips to visit their distant family members became harder and harder because of distance, their health and their age. They did travel to Pennsylvania when granddaughter Leslie Ann Simpson married in August 1968. And they attempted to attend granddaughter Doris Jean Crisler's wedding to Larry Campbell in 1970, but were thwarted by a significant Chicago blizzard. They especially enjoyed visits from their children and grandchildren and made exceptional efforts to show them the sights of central Florida including beach trips and even day trips to Orlando's Disney World. I fondly remember taking my three young children, David, age five, Jennifer, age three and Scott, almost two years old, to visit them in 1976. My sister, Lauran, accompanied us on this trip during her spring break from college. Orval was insistent that the children (his great grandchildren) should go to Disney World. Getting up early one weekday morning, he drove us from Dunedin to Orlando, an hour and a half one-way drive, accompanied us throughout the park, then drove all of the tired grand-children and great grandchildren home to Dunedin after a full day. Looking back on this memory I am amazed that an 83 year old man had the stamina to keep up with us. But he did and 'in spades'. What a wonderful memory of a remarkable effort on his part!

Orval Crisler with great grandsons David and Scott Fetterman and granddaughter Lauran Simpson. February 1976

In the early 1980s, granddaughter Cathleen Seefeldt took her first nursing job in Florida. Cathy had graduated from Elmhurst College (in suburban Chicago) with her bachelor's degree in nursing and moved to Florida not far from Orval and Jennie's home in Dunedin. The Crislers were pleased to have a family member so close and enjoyed seeing their granddaughter when she had time away from her new job. Cathy's parents, Emily and Lyle, were more frequent visitors to Florida with their only daughter, as well as Emily's parents, living in Florida.

Health issues would begin to plague both of them, but Jennie, in particular, as they aged. Jennie was diagnosed with hypertension (high blood pressure), heart disease and diabetes. Orval had bouts of arthritis, gout and tendonitis that made him uncomfortable and in 1982 (at age 89) he resorted to hiring someone to help him with his yard work. Rather than writing an individual letter to each of his five children Orval took to writing one letter which he would copy and send to each of his five children to keep them informed of family news on a regular basis. These letters were filled with mention of doctor's visits and hospitalizations, but despite that were amazingly upbeat in outlook.

In the mid 1980s, health issues would become more challenging for both Orval and Jennie and self-care was no longer workable. Son John and daughter-in-law June made arrangements to bring Orval and Jennie back to the Chicago area to their home in West Chicago to help care for them. Orval died in January 1986 following a brief illness and hospitalization. Jennie would follow him in June 1986. According to their instructions and desires, following their funerals in the Chicago area, they were both taken back to Rensselaer, Indiana for burial near Jennie's father, William Cyrus Comer and Orval's parents, William Addison and Minnie Delilah Crisler in Weston Cemetery.

Chapter 6

Glasgow Scotland at the Turn of the Twentieth Century

My paternal grandparents, James and Jeanie Thomson Russell Simpson, were natives of Glasgow, Scotland, both born in the 1890s. They emigrated to the United States in the mid 1920s with my father, their only son, Leslie Alexander Simpson. Since both of my grandparents and my father died before I became interested in researching my family genealogy, I do not have as much specific information on their early lives. By painting a picture of Glasgow, Scotland at the turn of the twentieth century I hope to provide an idea of what their early lives were like.

Both of the families of James and Jeanie were residents of Glasgow, Scotland and both of their fathers at the time of their births were employed in one of the largest and most important industries in the city—shipbuilding. Glasgow, situated on the banks of the River Clyde on the west coast of Scotland, twenty miles from the mouth of the river was an ideal setting for shipbuilding. Shipbuilding, along with locomotive manufacturing for the expanding railway system in the British Isles and growing expertise in engineering for these two industries, had caused Glasgow to grow in the latter part of the nineteenth century. The Industrial Revolution brought people from the rural areas of Scotland to the cities and between 1740 and 1840 Glasgow's population jumped tenfold.[114] The Glasgow environs provided an ideal setting for these industries, especially after the Clyde was deepened and widened in the early parts of the 1800s. The nearby fields of Lanarkshire surrounding the city were rich in iron ore for making iron and steel. Generous coal fields close by the city were mined and provided fuel for the industries and residents. Enhanced by a developing rail network, the nearby Monkland Canal provided a cheap and easy water route to the city.

A ready workforce already existed in Glasgow where in the early 1800s Glaswegian industrialists had expanded their manufacturing base, particularly in soap-making, distilling, glass-making, sugar and textiles. [115] By the latter part of the 1800s, Glasgow had developed into a great industrial city and trading port. As it grew and expanded it started referring to itself as the 'second city of the Empire', second to London. In 1864 there were more than twenty shipyards in the Glasgow area and by 1900 there were forty-five shipyards employing 28,000 workers, eighty percent of them skilled craftsmen. By 1870 more than half the British shipbuilding workforce was based on the River Clyde. Industries in Glasgow and the surrounding towns produced one-fifth of Britain's steel, one-third of its shipping tonnage, half the marine horse power, a third of the railroad rolling stock, and almost all of the sewing machines. Manufacturing firms in the city of Glasgow provided the engines, the boilers, the brass, copper and wooden fittings as well as the sometimes lavish furnishings for ships built further downstream on the Clyde.

Clydebank, a suburb to the west and further downstream from downtown Glasgow, allowed the shipbuilders to launch larger ships than could be built in the narrow reach of the Clyde further up-river. Clydebank grew out of the housing built in Radnor Park by Thomson's Ship Yard, opened in 1871. It was officially founded as a police burgh in 1886. [116] Clydebank was the home of two major ship yards—Thomsons and W. W. Beardmore.

In 1812, Europe's first sea-going steam ship, *The Comet,* was launched at Port Glasgow. [117] The legendary Glasgow-built *Cutty Sark,* launched in 1869, became one of the fastest sailing ships in the world, making record times between Britain and Australia. In the twentieth century Clydebank became world famous for the construction of ocean-going liners such as the *Queen Mary, Queen Elizabeth and Queen Elizabeth II.* [118] In 1906, the *Lusitania*, a British luxury ocean liner was launched from the John Brown Company's Glasgow shipyard. The *Lusitania* met a disastrous end as a casualty of the First World War when she was torpedoed by a German submarine in 1915. The great ship sank in just eighteen minutes killing 1,198 of the people aboard. The sinking of the *Lusitania* turned public opinion in many countries against Germany. It is often considered by historians to be the second most famous civilian passenger liner disaster after the sinking of *Titanic*. Interestingly, the *Titanic* was not Clyde built. It was built in Belfast, Ireland and Glaswegians often commented that if she had been built on the Clyde she would not have sunk. At the turn of the twentieth century the term 'Clyde-built' became synonymous with quality products of which the Glaswegian workers were justifiably proud. Glasgow ship-builders were acknowledged worldwide as supreme masters of the building of ships and the powering of them with steam engines of ever increasing efficiency.[119]

In 1900, Glasgow had a population of approximately one million inhabitants. The name Glasgow is derived from the Celtic Glas Gau, meaning 'Green Glen' or 'dear green place'. [120] Glaswegians proudly saw their city as the 'most progressive city in the world'. Between 1870 and 1914, Glasgow ranked as one of the richest and finest cities in Europe. The city boasted more municipal services than any other city of its size. In the late 1850s Queen Victoria had approved the Loch Katrine Scheme which brought fresh water from the nearby Trossachs to the city and vir-tually eliminated the disease typhus which had claimed many lives due to contaminated water supplies. Slum clearance, gas supply, public lighting, tramways, libraries, museums and parks all made Glasgow's occupants proud of their city's services.

In addition to the shipbuilding and locomotive manufacturing indus-tries some Glaswegians were employed by the American Singer sewing machine company. Beginning in the 1850s this manufacturing enter-prise transformed the production of apparel. The new machines were built in a custom built facility that opened in Clydebank, a Glasgow suburb, in the 1880s, producing approximately ten thousand machines each week. Initially, the hand and foot-powered Singer machine allowed home clothes-making to persist, but with the arrival of electrical power, factory production of ready-to-wear clothes began to expand. The Singer plant in Clydebank would experience declining demand for its product but would remain open until its closure in 1984. The use of the sewing machine allowed the Scottish cotton-thread making firms of J. and J. Clark and J. and P. Coats to expand, until they controlled eighty percent of the world's trade in thread. [121] Today all seamstresses and home sewers the world over are familiar with the thread made by the merged company today known as Coats and Clark.

Working middle class inhabitants of Glasgow like the Simpsons and the Russells lived in tenement apartment houses. The tenements built in Glasgow between 1870 and 1914 were an ideal way to house the rapidly growing population during Glasgow's industrial expansion in the latter half of the nineteenth century. In fact, between 1872 and 1876, more than 21,000 tene-ment houses were constructed in Glasgow. Little thought was given to their outward appearance, and the decoration, if any, consisted largely of variations in window design, with plain windows broken up by an occasional bay window.[122] The tenement building provided accommodation for many families on the minimum of valuable building land, and it could be adapted to suit the incomes of different social classes. However, the crowded tenements often became a breeding ground for contagious disease.

In working class areas, most tenement flats had only two rooms ("room and kitchen" flats) or even only one room (the "single-end" flat). At the turn of the twentieth century seventy five percent of all tenement flats in Glasgow were either room and kitchen houses or single-ends. Single-ends were often inhabited by young married couples or the elderly. Apartments with two rooms, kitchen and bathroom, were built for the slightly better-off or for larger families. For even wealthier people, there were larger flats with four, five or even more rooms.

Home of Alexander and Mary Simpson in Glasgow as it appeared in 1995

Home of Adam and Helen Russell in Glasgow as it appeared in 1995

Glasgow tenements were built in white or red sandstone and usually had three or four floors, with two or more separate flats on each floor.[123] Sandstone, a common building and paving material, is the most common building material within the city of Glasgow including the buildings of Glasgow University, many of the city's monuments and most of the apartment buildings. Most tenement occupants were renters who paid monthly rent to a landlord.

It is unknown how large the actual flats were where our ancestors lived. However, from the literature it is known that it was not uncommon for families of seven or eight people or more to all live in the small two room apartments at this time and it can be surmised that our ancestors, both the Simpson and Russell families, lived in small two-room apartments in their Glasgow tenements. It may be hard for us to fathom today how so many family members could live so closely in such small spaces but somehow they managed and there were advantages including family closeness and a strong sense of community. New babies were welcomed by a large extended family as well as 'close' neighbors, children within each building were watched over by all of their neighbors, mothers had their sisters, mothers and other relatives close-by to support and assist them through difficult times, and ailing elderly residents were cared for by neighbors and near-by family.

In Scotland, the term 'tenement' lacks the uncomplimentary connotation it carries in other parts of the world, and refers simply to any block of apartments that share a common central staircase and lack an elevator, particularly those constructed prior to 1919. Tenements were, and continue to be, inhabited by a wide range of social classes and income groups. During the nineteenth century tenements became the predominant type of new housing in Scotland's industrial cities. Before World War I almost seventy percent of Glasgow families lived in tenement houses. They were constructed in terraces of tenements, and each entrance shared by a group of apartments was referred to as a *close* or *stair*—both referring to the shared passageway to the individual flats. The entrance lobby (close) and stair were often lined to shoulder height with colorful tiles and became known as 'wally closes'. Most 'wally closes' in Glasgow tenement apartment buildings did not have a door and were open to the outside and therefore were not locked. [124] Flights of stairs and landings were generally designated common areas, and residents traditionally took turns to sweep clean the floors of the shared areas. Building occupants also shared laundry facilities in the 'back green' (garden or yard). [125] Tenement houses built in the 1890s and later may have had improved facilities with bathrooms with running water. This, however, was cold water only. Hot water had to be heated on the kitchen range. A kitchen range fueled with coal provided cooking facilities and gas was available for lights.

Most tenement apartments had built in beds referred to as 'recess beds', 'set-in' beds or 'hole in the wall' beds. There was usually one built-in bed in the 'single end' type flat and in the 'room and kitchen' flat, one bed in the kitchen and one in the main room. There were no separate rooms just for sleeping in the Glasgow tenement apartments. Since space was at such a premium in the Glasgow tenement even the area beneath the 'hole in the wall' bed was utilized. Often a chest (kist) or a tin bath were stored beneath the bed. Mattresses were usually made from feather or straw (called a donkey's breakfast mattress) and a curtain was often across the front of the opening for some privacy. Additional bedding could also be stored there during the day when not in use for sleeping. In large families sleeping arrangements could be problematic. It was not uncommon for young babies to actually sleep in dresser drawers. Older babies would graduate to a 'cot' (crib). Older children often shared a single bed, as many as two at the top and two at the bottom. In cold weather with no central heating numerous children in a bed had the advantage of keeping each other warm. 'Stone piggies' (hot water bottles) could be used to warm up the bed. I remember Grandpa Simpson (James) telling me that as a child he did not have heat in the room where he slept at night and when it was cold he had to stay warm with numerous blankets and quilts piled on top of him. Since he was the eldest of twelve children he probably had to sleep with some of his younger brothers.

Many apartments built before the turn of the twentieth century were built with bed closets, beds in large cupboards with a door. However, in 1900, health concerns, particularly pulmonary tuberculosis, drove the need for improved ventilation. Confined spaces such as the recessed bed cupboard were outlawed by the Glasgow Building Regulation Act. It decreed that '*No dwelling house shall contain an enclosed bed or a bed recess which is not open in front for three quarters of its length, and from floor to ceiling*'. Existing tenements had to be brought into compliance with this ruling within five years. [126]

In the kitchen the cast-iron sink was most often on the outside wall overlooking the 'back green' with one cold water tap and no hot water. The tap was made of brass in a swan-neck shape. A coal bunker with a hinged lid could hold approximately two hundred pounds of coal for the black cast-iron range. Coal was delivered regularly by a vendor in a house-drawn cart. The range often had a compartment for heating water. If not, water had to be boiled in large cast-iron kettles and pots on top of the range. There was also a food press and a pot press, a set of drawers and two long shelves.

In addition, all kitchens had a pulley for drying clothes in inclement weather. The pulley, a sort of clothes horse, was suspended from the middle of the ceiling by ropes and pulleys. Clothes could be hung and dried over the heat from the kitchen range when there was rain in the 'back green'. Rain in Glasgow is not an uncommon occurrence with monthly amounts of twelve to thirteen inches routinely. An expandable pine table usually occupied the middle of the small kitchen and was surrounded by simple wooden chairs and stools. In large families children had to take turns at the kitchen table since not all could be seated at the same time because of crowding.

The floor was usually covered with linoleum, some extravagantly patterned. Linoleum, a floor covering made from solidified linseed oil in combination with wood flour or cork dust over burlap or canvas backing became popular as an affordable floor covering in the latter part of the nineteenth century. Developed by an Englishman, the Scots became the largest producer of linoleum in 1877 when the Scottish town of Kirkcaldy in Fife boasted six linoleum manufacturers. [127]

Most tenements houses were remarkably similar in their layout and arrangement of individual flats. The shared 'close', or entrance passageway, led to stairs to the upper 'houses' and through to the shared back court/back green where the communal wash-house resided. A typical house had twelve flats and the occupants 'up oor close' made a little community. Neighbors shared rotating responsibilities (referred to as 'rota', a British term for a fixed order of rotation) for cleaning shared toilets, using the wash-house in the back court, and cleaning the common areas.

As families grew in size with the birth of additional babies families would often move to larger flats in the same close or across the street in order to maintain proximity with their family and friends. This was true for James and Jeanie Simpson in their early years of marriage in the early 1920s when they lived in a tenement house that was 'back to back' with Jeanie's family. They shared the same back court when James and Jean with their infant Leslie lived on Hutton Drive and her parents, Adam and Helen Russell, lived on the next street over, Drive Road. Jeanie would have been able to cross the back court to her mother's flat without going 'around the block'.

Housework for the Glasgow tenement housewife was no easier than for the Indiana farmwife in the years before the turn of the century. At the time of their births in the 1890s ,James and Jeanie's mothers' days were filled from dawn to dusk (and sometimes later) managing the household without the modern conveniences we take for granted today. There was no electricity, no central heat, no water heater, no vacuum cleaner, and no refrigerator. Most apartments had no indoor toilet. Several families often shared one toilet (called a 'cludgie'), built outside at the back of the building and at night would have to use a chamber pot. [128] In other tenements two families would share a toilet placed on the half landing between floors. In 1917 only seven percent of Glasgow one room flats had a toilet and only thirty-eight percent of two room flats had a toilet.

Lighting during often dreary Glasgow rainy and overcast days was provided by dim gaslights whose delicate and fragile mantle were easily torn when the lamp was lit. Each household had to maintain extra mantles on hand at all times. Gas lights would hiss and smell and were not as bright as electric lights. Most Glasgow tenements did not become electrified until after World War II (after 1945). And even though there was often limited sunshine the rooms were often painted in dark colors so they would not show the dirt caused by coal fires. The only available heat in the small one or two room tenement flats was provided by the coal range which became the center of the household in all seasons.

Shopping was done daily in the neighborhood since there was no refrigeration for storing food. Laundry was a time consuming task that could only be done as per the rotation schedule with other neighbors in the tenement, usually once every eight to twelve days, depending on how many neighbors shared the back court. Mothers with small infants resorted to hand laundering their infants 'nappies' (diapers) and clothing in their kitchen on a daily basis.

Let's look a little closer at the work of the Glasgow housewife at the turn of the twentieth century. A major challenge for any Glaswegian housewife at this time in the working class neighborhood was adequately feeding her family on an often limited budget. Meals were plain and simple and food was usually fresh because of the lack of refrigeration. Meats, usually beef, lamb, chicken for special occasions, and sometimes rabbit were often prepared in soups and stews to economically serve all family members. Sometimes cheese, fresh fish (haddock, cod or halibut) or kippers were used as additional protein sources. Kippers, salted and smoked herring fish, were commonly served as breakfast food in place of bacon or sausage. Vegetables, particularly potatoes, cabbage, turnips, carrots, onions and leeks were staples and eaten regularly. Other staples included porridge (oatmeal) cooked with milk or cream, and bread with jam or marmalade. Recipes were often handed down from mother to daughter and certain foods were associated with particular occasions and holidays. Jeanie Simpson enjoyed preparing Steak and Kidney Pie and Mince and Tatties (potatoes). Steak and Kidney Pie is a main course pie of beef steak and beef kidneys in a rich meat gravy and covered with a rich pastry topping. Mince is a common dish even today in Scottish households and consists of ground beef, onion, and carrots sautéed together with some additional ingredients, a typical comfort food much like Shepherd's Pie. Jeanie Simpson, since she did not personally like onion, avoided adding onion to her mince.

Bread was purchased daily from the bakery and this was often a chore for the young boys of the household who were sent to the neighborhood bakery to pick up the family's bread for the day. Scotland had a fine tradition of baking and bakeries were common in all Glasgow neighborhoods. In addition, many housewives took pride in their home-baking including a variety of scones and oatcakes. Scones (the Scottish equivalent of the baking powder biscuit) were often prepared at least twice a week by the housewife for tea-time and served with marmalade and clotted cream. Clotted cream is a thick yellow cream made by heating raw (or unpasteurized) cow's milk and then leaving it in a shallow pan for several hours until the cream content rises to the surface and forms 'clots'. It is typically used throughout the United Kingdom and forms the basis for 'cream tea'. [129]The word scone, pronounced like con or John, not cone and Joan, is pronounced differently in various parts of the United Kingdom. According to one source, ninety-nine percent of the Scottish population uses the 'con or John' pronunciation along with two-thirds of the British population. [130] Our Scottish relatives always used the 'con or John' pronunciation when referring to this Scottish quick bread.

Since many Glaswegian families had come to the city from the rural areas of the country seeking work they brought with them cooking and baking traditions which utilized familiar grains like oats and barley. Our Scottish families were no exception. Jeanie Simpson made a delicious oatmeal dressing for stuffing roast chicken which continues to be a family favorite today. She also prepared a delicious chicken soup with barley, rather than rice, potato, or noodles.

Dairy products, milk, cream and butter were usually delivered regularly from a local dairy by hand-pushed or horse-pulled carts. Farmers brought fresh milk straight from their farms outside the city via horse drawn cart and delivered it to a neighborhood dairy in a five-gallon churn in the early morning hours. Housewives would either go the neighborhood dairy or wait for home delivery. Each housewife purchased only as much milk as she could utilize within the next day or two. Small milk cans or jugs were taken out to the cart by the housewife or her 'messenger' (usually a child) and milk was poured from the churn into the household's personal jug. Prior to refrigerators some housewives would utilize a piece of marble, called a 'cold slab' where she set her perishable dairy products like milk and butter. Others set their perishables in a bowl of cool water or in a deep sink. But this was only good for a day or two before the products went bad. Milk at this time was not pasteurized and had a limited shelf life without refrigeration.

Meat was purchased from the butcher, fish from the fish monger, groceries from the grocer, vegetables and fruit from the greengrocer. All of these vendors could be found in each Glasgow neighborhood. Many vendors had their businesses in ground floor shops and the shopkeeper and his family lived in a small apartment (flat) either behind or above the shop.

In most Scottish households porridge was a weekday staple along with toasted bread and jam or marmalade for breakfast. Porridge, the Scottish term for what we refer to as oatmeal, was prepared with milk or cream. They never added raisins, cinnamon or other fruits. Most Scottish and Irish housewives used steel cut oats rather than the rolled oats that were commonly used in the United States and England. Since steel cut oatmeal required a longer cooking time, up to twenty to thirty minutes, many women would start their porridge before retiring for bed at night, then warm it up in the morning. Eggs with ham, sausage, bacon or kippers, and potato scones, known as a full English breakfast or fried breakfast, was usually reserved for Sunday mornings.

Since fresh fish was plentiful in a country surrounded by an ocean it was a frequent addition to the dinner or tea-time table in Glasgow. Haddock, herring or cod were the usual varieties. Cod and haddock were often dried and then grilled with butter or stewed with milk and onions for a delicately flavored fish stew. Jeanie Simpson enjoyed preparing Finnan Haddie, a traditional Scottish recipe utilizing smoked fish. Smoked fish had a history in Scotland going back to the sixteenth century. In the late nineteenth century, after faster transportation via Scottish rail improved transport, it became easier to move fresh and smoked fish from the sea to the Scottish cities including Edinburgh and Glasgow. When the Aberdeen fishing village of Findon (pronounced locally as "Finnan") began producing lightly smoked and delicately flavored haddock (haddies) it had a ready market in the city. Just as in England, fish and chips was a popular eat-out meal for most Glaswegians. In fact, fish and chip shops were one of the few restaurants that working class folks frequented. For many tenement residents, a fish and chips supper was a Friday evening treat after a long work-week. James Simpson referred to going to the infrequent trip to the 'chippie' for fish and chips as a special treat.

Scottish sweets or desserts were most often reserved for holidays or special occasions. Clootie dumpling, a traditional Scottish pudding is an example. It is a pudding named after the cloth (or cloot) in which it was cooked. Usually made with flour, currants, sultanas (raisins made from Thompson seedless grapes), treacle (similar to molasses), sugar, suet (beef or mutton fat), orange peel, and spices. Following mixing the pudding was wrapped in a cloth, placed on a plate in a large pot of water and boiled for two hours before serving. Although I don't remember my grandfather or father mentioning Clootie dumpling specifically I do remember my father particularly enjoying Crosse and Blackwell's Plum Pudding (very similar to Clootie dumpling, I believe) with a warm lemon sauce at Christmas. He also enjoyed mincemeat pie, a rich and aromatic mixture of English Pippin apples, raisins, and spices.

Marzipan candy was another European treat that the Simpsons enjoyed. Marzipan, a confection of ground almonds and sugar, is mixed, then formed into small bite-sized shapes, like vegetables or fruits, and painted with food colorings. It is particularly popular in Europe, especially at holiday seasons like Christmas and Easter and probably had its origin in Germany in the fifteenth century. [131]

Mealtimes in the working class areas of Glasgow were often dictated by the schedules of the shipyard workmen and the 'horns' that signaled the beginning and ending of their work days. Breakfast was usually eaten between 7 and 8 AM. The midday meal, called dinner, was served between 12 noon and 1 PM when school age children and some workmen who lived close enough came home for their mid-day meal. Tea was served shortly after 5 PM in the evening. In many families it was customary for the father to eat first, before his wife and children. The father, the wage-earner, usually got the choicest servings, while the mother was always the last to eat and often was short-changed on serving size. The mother looked after the family first and was last to get what there was. [132] In large families two sittings were customary with the adults eating first and the children eating later.

Beside food preparation the Glasgow housewife had a full-time job (six to seven days a week) maintaining her small tenement apartment. Standards of cleanliness were extremely high. According to Jean Faley in 'Up Oor Close', "scrupulous cleanliness made a clear social statement about respectability, and women slaved long hours to maintain it. Door brasses must be shining, children washed and decently clothed. But small houses could be made to gleam with concerted effort, and this was a source of pride and pleasure to most women and their families".[133] Jeanie Simpson exemplified her earlier domestic training in Glasgow after she had moved to the United States. Her daughter-in-law, Virginia Simpson, remembers that Jeanie's morning routine included sweeping her kitchen floor every day and when she scrubbed her kitchen floor she always got down on her hands and knees to scrub it thoroughly.

In the Glasgow tenement apartment without running hot water, a large kettle of water was always kept simmering over the fire on the black kitchen range. Hand washing, socks and undergarments, and 'nappies' if there was an infant in the household, was done daily. The big wash was done in the shared wash-house in the rear close and was a full day's work by itself. Ironing was another time-consuming chore, done with a flat iron heated on the kitchen range. Irons were used in pairs, one heating on the stove while the other was in use. The process of laundering and ironing could consume one or two full days for the Glasgow housewife.

The heart of the home, the kitchen range provided warmth, hot water and the means of cooking. It, however, required constant attention. In most Glasgow households the range had to be blackened and burnished regularly, most likely weekly on a Friday evening. Black leading came in a packet which was broken up and mixed with water. It was applied to the range with a brush, allowed to dry and burnished (polished) with a small square of velvet until it gleamed black and shiny, not without a lot of 'elbow grease'.[134] The range had to be fed with coal from a bunker in the kitchen several times a day. This created layers of dust and grime which had to be constantly removed. The kitchen range did have the advantage of being able to burn household rubbish and trash that did not have to be carted back to the midden in the rear close for disposal. [135]

Carpets had to be taken outside to the rear close to be beaten with a rug beater, sometimes up and down several flights of stairs. Linoleum flooring was scrubbed on hands and knees. Shared toilets and the 'wally close' were scrubbed on a rotating weekly basis with families sharing the responsibility. Children were expected to help out with the household chores, girls more so than the boys. The boys typically were sent out to run errands (messengers), beat the rugs in the close, cut up newspaper for toilet paper, cut paper tapers from newspaper to light their father's pipes and polish their father's work boots. The girls helped with the lighter cleaning chores, did the dishes, and watched the younger children. Mothers did the heavier cleaning.

Friday evenings, customarily a time devoted to cleaning the house prior to the weekend, involved the mother and her children in an intensive round of thorough cleaning, a miniature spring cleaning. The grate was done, the hearth was done, the table was scrubbed, the cupboards were done". [136] At the conclusion of a Friday evening cleaning many Glaswegian families treated themselves to a fish and chips supper from the neighborhood 'chip shop'. Their apartment was ready for Saturday and Sunday, the days for visiting and being visited and for cooking a special Sunday meal and possibly church and Sunday school. Most children in this primarily Protestant country attended Sunday School.

The weekly laundry was a job for the housewife which demanded a huge time and labor commitment. Most women shared the use of the wash house in the rear close. The rear close was a busy communal place that provided space for a shared wash house, a place for drying clothes on clothes lines strung between the apartments, a place to beat rugs and carpets, and the 'midden' for rubbish. 'Midden ' was the Scottish word used to designate a dump for domestic waste. Most rear closes were paved over while some of the slightly better tenements had a little grassy area as well. All provided a safe environment where children could play in view of their mothers who overlooked the rear close from their kitchen windows.

Starting early in the morning (sometimes as early as 4 or 5 AM) the Glasgow housewife would go to the wash house and start a wood fire under a large copper boiler filled from a hose attached to a cold water tap. It would take several hours for the water to heat up. Many women would start the fire and return to their homes to prepare breakfast for their husbands and children before returning to the warm water in the wash house to proceed with the day's laundry chores. Carbolic soap, a mild disinfectant soap with a distinctive odor, was commonly used. In addition to the copper boiler, the wash house contained large sinks where the clothes would be scrubbed on a metal scrub board and a wringer or mangle to squeeze the water out of the washing before it was hung up in the back court. Clothes lines were stretched across the close between the buildings. A long fork was used to prop the line up high off the ground so that the clean laundry would not drag on the ground. [137] In inclement weather, wet clothes had to be returned to the apartment where they could be hung over the kitchen range using a clothes pulley.

The Glasgow housewife at the turn of the century took great pride in the appearance of her laundry. Much of the wash was white including shirts, blouses, night-shirts, underwear and bed linens. And much value was placed on laundry with a snowy white appearance. Bluing was used by most laundresses to provide a slightly blue tint that increased the impression of whiteness. 'Dolly Blue' bluing in the United Kingdom was similar to the American products, 'Mrs. Stewart's' or 'Little Boy Blue'. 'Dolly Blue' was packaged in little bags with a distinctive stick peeking out of the bundle.[138] Many whites were then starched with a product called 'Robin's Starch' which came in a packet and was dissolved in water to provide stiffness to shirts, collars, and linens prior to ironing.[139]

Scotland has a long history of universal provision of public education, and the Scottish education system is distinctly different from other parts of the United Kingdom. Scots were very proud of their 99 percent literacy rate, even as early as the 1900s. In 1872, it was the first nation to pass a compulsory education law for all children, followed by England in 1880. Between 1901 and 1945 Scottish children were required to stay in school until age 14. Those with academic ability could pursue a challenging range of academic subjects and gain a School Leaving Certificate on completion of their secondary education at age 16. Very few children of the Glasgow tenements, children of working class families, could expect to continue on to university studies. Since so many of their parents were employed in the industrial manufacturing companies of the city many, like our relative, James Simpson, pursued apprenticeship programs that allowed them to learn while on-the-job. James probably left school at either age 14 or 16 and following in his father's footsteps went to work in the shipbuilding industry where he was apprenticed as a wooden pattern maker.

Christmas in Scotland prior to World War II was unlike the commercial holiday it became in the latter years of the twentieth century. Shops did not close and workmen commonly were required to work on Christmas Day if it fell during the work week. If families gave presents to their children for Christmas it was usually a simple stocking filled with an apple or orange and a tuppence (two pennies) and hung by the kitchen stove or at the end of the bed at night, sometimes with a small toy like a flashlight (called a 'torch' in Scotland) or a mouth organ (harmonica). Christmas trees were a rarity in pre-World War II Glasgow. Christmas dinner was often centered around a roasted Christmas goose or chicken. Roast turkey was too much of a luxury for most working class families at the turn of the twentieth century.

The most anticipated holiday and the one that surpassed the Christmas festivities was New Years, called Hogmanay in Scotland. The origins of Hogmanay date back to pagan rituals that marked the time of the winter solstice. Roman celebrations of the winter festival of Saturnalia and Viking celebrations of Yule (the origin of the twelve days of Christmas) contributed to celebrations in Scotland around the New Year. New Year's Day was always the most important holiday for Scottish adults. All workers had several days off from work to allow them to bring in the New Year with the customary tradition of 'first-footing'. The custom known as 'first footing' dictates that the first person to cross a home's threshold after midnight on New Year's Eve will determine the homeowner's luck for the new year. The ideal visitor would bear gifts, preferably coal for the fire, small cakes, or a coin, and of course, whisky and should be a man with a dark complexion. The dark complexion relates back to the eighth century, when the presumably fair-haired Vikings invaded Scotland—a blond visitor was not a good omen. [140] Women could not be 'first-footers' since they were deemed to bring bad luck. In another tradition the back door of the house was opened just before midnight to let out the old year. As the new year began, the front door was opened to let it in.

Although the Glaswegians were hard-working people they made time for relaxation and entertainment. In the summer children spent a great deal of time outside often playing in the rear close watched over by their mothers while in the winter family members enjoyed reading, listening to stories, playing music and playing indoor games. Mothers would often sit mending clothes or doing hand-work. Without radio or television adults and children spent more time socializing in their homes with families and neighbors.

Since working fathers did not benefit from paid vacation days it was not uncommon for a mother to take her children to the beach for a day outing, 'doon the watter' (down the water). Nearby resorts like Largs, Dunnoon and the Isle of Bute could be reached from Glasgow by steamboat or train. We know that Jeanie Simpson would take her young son, Leslie, to the coastal town of Largs, west of Glasgow, with its beach at Millport during the summer. They probably traveled by train to go to Largs.

During the 1890s when James and Jeanie were young children, Glaswegians depended on horsepower to get around their city. Large Clydesdales were utilized to pull horse-drawn carts, carriages and horse-drawn buses and even a horse-drawn stagecoach in some areas of the city. Horse-drawn trams were operated by the Glasgow Tramway and Omnibus Company until 1903 when the trams were electrified. James and Jeanie were just eight to ten years old at the time. The new electrified trams were a definite improvement over the horse-drawn trams. Horses had to be housed, groomed, and cared for day in and day out. Their work day was limited to four or five hours a day and they typically could only pull a car for a dozen miles a day. Many systems needed ten or more horses in the stable for each horse-pulled tramcar. Electric trams, also called streetcars or trolleys, operated on a track system (similar to railroad tracks). Fares were one to three pence, depending on where the passenger boarded the tram. It is very likely that James's and Jeanie's fathers and later James all used the Glasgow tram system, both horse-drawn and electric tram, to get to their job in the shipyards where they were employed from their homes in the Govan district of Glasgow. Both families relied on public transportation and foot power to get around the city.

After the turn of the century motorized cars and buses made their appearance in Glasgow, but not without some concern by the citizenry. A newspaper report in 1910 mentioned vehicles speeding at over twelve miles per hour! [141] The development of the automobile in the United Kingdom including Scotland mirrored it's development in the United States and the rest of Europe. Grandfather James Simpson did not become an owner of an automobile until the late 1940s after he had moved to the United States and was a grown man of almost fifty.

Chapter 7

James Simpson

Glaswegians Alexander and Mary Stewart Simpson were proud parents when their first born son, James, was born May 20, 1893. Little James was not given a middle name. Prior to the twentieth century many Scottish families followed a particular naming tradition with the first born son usually named after the father's father, the second son after the mother's father. By the late 1800s many families were beginning to stray from this tradition and apparently the Simpsons exemplified that fact when baby James was not named Alexander after his father and his paternal grandfather. A later born son and younger brother to James, however, would be named Alexander.

James' parents, Alexander and Mary, were both from seafaring families who had moved to Glasgow in the late 1800s in search of work. Alexander Simpson's family hailed from the northeast coast of Scotland, a small fishing port called Lossiemouth in Morayshire (the Scottish county of Moray) and that is where Alexander Simpson and his siblings had been born. When the fishing industry was in a downturn around 1880, Alexander's father, also named Alexander, had moved his family to Glasgow. Mary Stewart, the daughter of Kenneth Stewart and Jane Thorburn, was born in Dumfries, in southern Scotland, just north of the English border. Her father had also moved to Glasgow with his family is search of employment. Alexander Simpson and Mary Stewart met and fell in love while living in Glasgow. They married in 1890 in Glasgow. Their first child, a daughter, named Jane was born in 1891. First born daughter Jane was named according to Scottish naming tradition after her mother's mother, Jane Thorburn.

In 1893 the young Simpson couple, Alexander and Mary, lived just one mile west of downtown Glasgow in the small burgh of Kinning Park, adjacent to the Govan/Ibrox community. In 1897 Kinning Park was a separate community outside of Glasgow with a population of approximately fourteen thousand. In the early years of 1900, Kinning Park, along with Govan and Ibrox would all be absorbed into the city limits of greater Glasgow. Its principal industries in the late 1800s were engineering, bread and biscuit baking, soap-making and paint-making. It was home to many artisans and laborers employed in its industries as well as shipbuilding in nearby communities along the River Clyde. [142]

James' father, Alexander Simpson, was a ship's engineer in the maritime industry centered in Glasgow while Mary, like most other Scottish women at that time, was a stay-at-home housewife and mother. Following Jane and James, Alexander and Mary's family would grow to twelve children. Their last child, Elizabeth was born in 1917. All of their children were raised in the working class tenements of Glasgow and the family moved several times within the city and its suburbs to find more commodious lodgings to accommodate their growing family.

Mary Simpson's babies were probably all born at home with the assistance of a midwife or family member in attendance. A physician would often stop by the home during a woman's labor or be called if there were problems with the birth. And although Glasgow had a maternity hospital as early as 1834, the Glasgow Royal Maternity Hospital, most women prior to 1948 (with the development of the British National Health Service) chose to give birth at home. At the turn of the twentieth century some women died in childbirth or soon after from puerperal, or childbirth, fever, particularly poor women who were malnourished. In many Glasgow families, it was commonplace to lose one baby or child in infancy. Following birth, most babies were breast fed for at least one year and many women saw breast feeding as a form of natural contraception. While the new mother was breast feeding she was less likely to become pregnant with another child. [143]

Contraception in the late 1800s and first part of the 1900s was frowned upon. While the Catholic church strongly forbade contraception, many Protestants also felt it was immoral and unnatural to do anything to prevent pregnancy. According to one source, there was a "kind of Calvinistic thing of non-interference with nature as far as contraception went". [144] That would explain why Protestant Mary Simpson was the mother of twelve 'weans' (Glaswegian term for children).

The possibility of infectious disease was always a concern for young parents and an inevitable part of life in the densely populated tenements. Before the advent of antibiotics, diphtheria, scarlet fever, meningitis, and tuberculosis were all possibly fatal diseases and children under age five were particularly susceptible. Only three out of one hundred people who contracted tuberculosis would survive. In 1900, one in five children died before age one.

A smallpox outbreak in Glasgow in 1894 must have been a great concern to Alexander and Mary with two young children, Jane and James. Despite the fact that smallpox vaccination had been developed by English physician Edward Jenner one hundred years previously smallpox was still taking lives at the turn of the twentieth century. Expanding trade networks as well as the rise of immigration and leisure travel meant that smallpox could spread more easily and more rapidly than ever before. Without vaccination smallpox was fatal for one in three of its victims and those that survived were often badly disfigured. [145] Smallpox, a serious, contagious, and sometimes fatal infectious disease still has no specific treatment. The only prevention is vaccination. The *pox* part of *smallpox* is derived from the Latin word for "spotted" and refers to the raised bumps that appear on the face and body of an infected person.[146]

Little James and his brothers and sisters would have started their schooling at age five in a Glasgow public school. The 1872 Scottish Education Act had dictated the compulsory attendance for all children aged five to thirteen. In 1883 the 'leaving age' was raised to age fourteen. The Scottish education system was quite different from other parts of the United Kingdom (England, Northern Ireland and Wales). The Scottish system emphasized breadth across a range of subjects while the rest of the United Kingdom countries emphasized greater depth of education. The curriculum centered around the basics of reading, writing and arithmetic. In addition to being compulsory, education was free, designed to ensure that young people could survive and make progress in any one of several occupations.[147]

From a letter written by Alexander Simpson to his young grandson, Leslie Simpson, in 1937, we know that James' parents, Alexander and Mary, did not benefit from the dictates of the 1872 law. In this letter Alexander mentions the fact that he left school at age eleven years and his wife Mary left school at age nine. We can assume that James and his siblings did benefit from the education legislation and attended school until they were at least fourteen years old and possibly sixteen years. It is likely that they attended the Govan Cross Public School when they were in school around the turn of the twentieth century. There students sat two to a desk, set up in a rigid line and bolted to the floor. Boys sat with boys, girls with girls. At age twelve students were required to take a qualifying exam, termed the "qualy". Those who passed the "qualy" moved up to "Senior Secondaries", others moved to establishments which taught metalwork and domestic science. The next divide was staying on for your "highers" or leaving at fourteen, and the last was going to the "Uni"(university) to become ministers, lawyers, teachers or the "Tech" (Royal Technical College) to be made into shipbuilders, mine managers, bridge builders, or textile managers.[148]

At that time most teachers in the lowers grades were women just as they were in the United States. Corporal punishment was utilized in Scottish schools when the Simpson children were students. Scottish schools in the early 1900s used the tawse to beat pupils on the palms. A tawse (the plural of Scots taw, a thong of a whip) is an implement for physical punishment, called tawsing. It was used for educational and domestic discipline. A tawse consists of a strip of leather, with one end split into a number of tails. The thickness of the leather and the number of tails varied. Many Scottish saddlers made tawses for local customers. Use of the tawse in Scottish schools was outlawed in 1986.[149]

Following completion of his elementary school education at age fourteen or sixteen James left school and entered an apprenticeship program as a wooden pattern maker in one of Glasgow's shipbuilding manufacturers. A pattern maker made models in wood to produce castings. These models were then used by a mold maker to form a cavity in the sand into which molten metal was poured to form a casting. Pattern makers had to be creative thinkers who were also good with their hands. They needed an eye for detail and have an understanding of the basic principles of the materials they were working with, specifically wood, iron and metal. They had to be able to understand and interpret engineering drawings, visualize the finished pattern in three dimensions and be especially good with mathematics, using accuracy and precision in making calculations.

In the early 1900s, when James was entering his profession, apprenticeships for the occupation of wooden pattern maker could take five to seven years of informal on-the-job training. During that time James worked a forty-eight hour work week with only one day off each week—Sunday. Scotland would not go to a forty-hour work week until 1919.[150] Many tradesmen in the shipbuilding and engineering industries, however, did not always appreciate steady employment. Workers could be laid-off at a moment's notice and upon showing up for work could find the gates closed and have no knowledge of when they would be needed again. There were virtually no permanent jobs as employment was dependent on contracts to build specific ships.[151]

It is unknown which specific shipyard or engineering firm employed James Simpson but according to his daughter-in-law, Virginia Simpson, James talked about working at Clydebank, several miles west and across the River Clyde from his home in Govan. Glasgow shipbuilding would reach its zenith in 1913, just prior to World War I, exactly when James was serving his apprenticeship as a pattern maker.[152] In 1913 the Clyde basin shipbuilders were producing twenty percent of the world's ships. The 'workshop of the Empire' flexed its muscles in preparation for war duty and the insatiable demand for munitions, machinery, steel and ships. Workers flocked to the Clyde to take advantage of full employment and abundant overtime. The Govan shipyards, Harland and Wolff, Ltd, Fairfield Shipbuilding and Engineering Company, Ltd, and Govan Shipbuilders, Ltd were producing a variety of ships including destroyers, battleships, passenger ferries and ocean-going vessels. In addition, a number of engineering firms and other manufacturing firms supported the Glasgow shipbuilders.

As James was getting his career as a wooden pattern maker started the Great War would increase the demands on the Glasgow shipbuilding industry at the same time that many shipyard employees, experienced managers and craftsmen, were enlisting in droves to fight for King and Country. During the years of the Great War (later called World War I) 1914-1918, the Admiralty took over management of the Glasgow shipyards. Orders for a variety of new ships including submarines and even a sea plane carrier were added work for the Glasgow shipyards. James was likely torn between enlisting and serving in the British forces during the war or staying in Glasgow and using his skills in support of the war effort. Since he was likely in the midst of the apprenticeship program he probably decided to stay and use his talents in the shipyards. We know that he did not serve in the British military during World War I.

Although the end of the First World War in late 1918 was welcomed it also heralded an era of uncertainty for the people of Glasgow and all of Scotland. Most dramatically in Glasgow, shipbuilding and heavy engineering soon slipped into recession. Naval orders were cancelled and men were laid off. Unemployment spread swiftly along Clydeside. By 1920 it was recognized that shipbuilding capacity had to be reduced, affecting first the steel industry and later shipbuilding and other industries that supported the shipyards.

The end of the war also brought changes to James Simpson when he made the big decision to marry. Twenty-six year old James had met and fallen in love with fellow Glaswegian twenty-four year old Jeanie Thomson Russell. Let's find out about Jeanie and her family.

Chapter 8

Jeanie Thomson Russell

Jeanie Thomson Russell was born at 10 Ingram Street (now called Wick Street) in Govan, a small burgh outside of Glasgow on March 26, 1895.[153] She was the second of five children born to Adam and Helen Stuart Russell. According to traditional Scottish naming patterns the first born daughter would be named after the maternal grandmother and the second born daughter after the paternal grandmother. Jeanie's older sister's name, Christina Castle Russell, followed the tradition and she was named after her maternal grandmother and namesake, Christina Castle. Most of us would think that if the naming tradition had been followed Jeanie should have been named Jane after her paternal grandmother, Jane Russell. However, since the names Jane and Jeanie are interchangeable in Scotland, the tradition was followed in her naming. It is not known where her middle name, Thomson, came from. However, her daughter-in-law, Virginia Simpson remembers quite clearly that Jeanie was quite proud of her middle name and maintained her middle name (rather than her maiden name) as a married woman. Her naturalization papers issued in 1941 reflect her name as Jeanie Thomson Simpson. Interestingly, the name Thomson is quite a significant and meaningful one in the history of Glasgow shipbuilding. The Thomson brothers, James and George, and George's two sons, James and George Thomson were instrumental in the development of major shipbuilding works on the banks of the River Clyde. I can't help but wonder if there is a connection between the shipbuilding Thomson family and the middle name of Jeanie Thomson Russell.

Jeanie's siblings included older sister Christina and younger siblings Adam (nicknamed Addie), Helen (nicknamed Nell), and Isabella. Jeanie's father, Adam Russell, was a Govan native. Her mother, Helen Stuart, was born in Ordiquhill, in the county of Banff, along the northeast coast of Scotland. Helen's father was a crofter (tenant farmer) in Banffshire and Helen had moved to Glasgow as a young woman to find employment as a domestic servant prior to her marriage to Adam Russell.

Crofter, a term used more often in the Highlands and islands of Scotland is used to designate a tenant who rents and cultivates a small holding of land or 'croft.' An Old English word, meaning originally an enclosed field, it may be related to the Dutch word 'kroft', a field on high ground or downs. The Crofters' Holdings (Scotland)Act of 1886, defined a crofter as the tenant of a holding who resides on his holding, the annual rent of which does not exceed thirty pounds in money, and which is situated in a crofting parish.[154]

From their earliest appearance the counties of Scotland were called "shires". The word "county" did not come into common usage until the nineteenth century. When James and Jeanie were born in the 1890s and between the years 1890 and 1975 there were 31 shires in Scotland, in addition to the islands of Orkney and Shetland. The cities of Glasgow, Edinburgh, Aberdeen, and Dundee had their own local governments, separate from the shires. Glasgow is located within the shire of Lanark, commonly referred to as Lanarkshire.

The Russell's home in Govan was located in the southwest portion of the city of Glasgow and two and half miles west of the city center. During the second half of the nineteenth century Govan underwent a massive transformation. It changed from what one prominent Scottish clergyman in 1851 called 'a picturesque and. rural village' to become the fifth largest burgh in Scotland. It was known as 'the shipbuildingest burgh in the world.' [155] In the eighteenth and nineteenth centuries weaving and coal mining were important and in the early nineteenth century shipbuilding emerged as Govan's principal industry. Historically, it was a working class neighborhood. In 1864, Govan gained burgh status and in 1901 it was the seventh largest town in Scotland. It was incorporated into the city of Glasgow in 1912.[156]

At the time of Jeanie's birth, her father was employed as a journeyman shipwright. The term shipwright was used in the latter part of the 1800s to denote a shipbuilder, a carpenter skilled in ship construction and repair. As a journeyman shipwright he would have been employed in one of the shipbuilding companies along the River Clyde in or near Glasgow. Helen, as other Glaswegian wives, was a housewife whose primary responsibility was keeping her house and nurturing her five children.

The Russells, like other working class Glasgow families, including the Simpsons, were tenement apartment dwellers. It is unknown what size apartment they occupied or how many times they moved within the Glasgow area. However, we do know that the Russells lived in Govan during their daughter Jeanie's growing up years and were living there when she married in 1919. Jeanie would have attended a Glasgow city school starting at age five and probably continued her education until she was fourteen years of age before leaving. After leaving school Jeanie became a tailoress/seamstress (typically called a sempstress in the United Kingdom). Apparently that is how she supported herself until she married James Simpson when she was twenty-four years of age. Little is known about this period of her life, particularly whether or not she was employed in a shop or another place of employment. She may have worked from her parent's home. In Glasgow only six percent of women were employed outside the home at that time.[157]

Jeanie Thomson Russell circa1915

Little is known of the courtship (commonly called 'coortin' or 'wooin' in Scotland) of James and Jeanie. They lived within a mile of each other, she in the area of Glasgow called Govan, he in neighboring Ibrox. They could have met at church or through mutual friends. It is very likely that James would have formally asked Jeanie's parents for their permission to marry. We know that James presented a diamond engagement ring to Jeanie prior to their marriage, a narrow band with five small diamonds. Scottish parents had generally more to say about marriages during this period. Marriage between like religious backgrounds and like socioeconomic backgrounds was expected and the norm. It was expected that a young man would at least inform the girl's parents of his intentions. As a prospective bride it would have been expected that Jeanie had a collection of bed-linens, blankets, table linens and bedroom furnishings to take to her new home. By the early 1900s dowries were still common in the more rural areas of Scotland when a crofter would be expected to provide a few sheep, cattle or money to the groom at the time of the marriage but probably not in the larger cities of Edinburgh or Glasgow.

Prior to their wedding date on Friday, June 27, 1919 'banns' were read for three consecutive Sundays in Jeanie's home church of St. Kenneth's Linthouse Church in Govan. In Scotland, 'marriage banns', commonly referred to as 'banns', were the public announcement in the church during a regular Sabbath service that a marriage was going to take place between a bride and groom. The practice of reading the 'marriage banns' originated in the medieval church of the thirteenth century and lasted for more than six centuries in Scotland. In later centuries, an alternative was to give notice and obtain a license to marry from a civil registrar. This method eventually became accepted by the Church of Scotland. Today, the practice of 'marriage banns' has declined, but giving notice has become compulsory for all regular marriages. [158]

James Simpson and Jeanie Russell were married in a private ceremony in the bride's home at 14 Drive Road in Govan, Glasgow by Reverend Samuel Knox, a minister of the United Free Church of Scotland and pastor of Jeanie's church, St. Kenneth's. The practice of home weddings was quite common in Glasgow at that time. Witnesses to the wedding were James Inglis and Helen (Nell) Russell, Jeanie's younger sister. The marriage was registered with the civil authorities in the Register Book for Marriages for the District of Govan in the County of Lanark.

Wedding Photo of James and Jeanie Simpson June 1919

During the interwar years (1918-1939) marriages were usually simple affairs among most Glasgow tenement families. It was customary for working class families along the west coast of Scotland including Glasgow to have a 'Penny Wedding' where guests were expected to bring their own food (pot-luck dishes) and drinks to the church or hall to celebrate after the ceremony was over. Most likely James and Jeanie shared their wedding ceremony with their immediate family members and then celebrated with a wedding meal and cake at her parent's home, possibly a 'Penny Wedding'. The wedding cake was most likely a fruit cake covered with icing with small trinkets baked in. Better off families would have a 'free wedding' when they would hire a local hall, a caterer, and musicians. Most weddings, both 'penny' and 'free' were 'dry', without alcoholic beverages. Couples usually wore their best clothes, the man a suit and the bride her best dress which would later become her Sunday dress. Although Queen Victoria had introduced the custom of wearing a white wedding dress, most brides did not commonly wear white until after the second World War. Any color was appropriate except for green, associated with fairies, and black, associated with mourning. For many couples, the celebratory meal following their wedding ceremony took the place of a honeymoon.

Friends and relatives provided presents to help the couple set up housekeeping. Prior to the wedding ceremony it was common for the bride's mother to host a 'show of presents' when everyone came to the bride's home to view the wedding gifts. This was particularly a West of Scotland/Glasgow custom.[159] The wedding tradition of "something old, something new, something borrowed, something blue" was commonly adhered to by Glasgow brides. Most wore a blue garter, symbolizing love and in some areas it was common for the bride to put a penny in her shoe to bring her good luck. [160] Sprigs of Scottish white heather (more rare than the purple heather) were often worn by the bride. And it was not uncommon to give a pot of white heather to the bride and groom to be placed near the door to ensure marital harmony.

Following the wedding most Glaswegian couples either lived with their parents or if they were lucky enough to have their own place, many started out their married lives in a one-room (single-end) apartment in a tenement. It is possible that James carried Jeanie over the threshold of their new home. This common custom was to avoid the bad luck of the bride tripping on her way in which would bring bad luck to the union. Another source indicated that the ancient tradition of carrying the bride over the doorstep was linked to the superstition that evil spirits inhabit the thresholds of doors. We do not know for sure whether James and Jeanie had their own apartment but certainly by the time their son, Leslie, was born in 1922, they did.

Chapter 9
Simpson Couple—The Early Years

The Simpson's only child, a son, Leslie Alexander Simpson, was born August 19, 1922 [161]after his parents had been married for three years. The family made their home at 5 Hutton Drive in the Govan area of Glasgow, south of the River Clyde, just around the corner from her parents, Adam and Helen Russell.

Home of James and Jeanie Simpson in Glasgow as it appeared in 1995

His parents, Alexander and Mary Simpson. lived in near-by Ibrox, a short distance away. Jeanie gave birth at home, probably with a midwife in attendance. Her baby boy, Leslie Alexander, was an unusually large infant weighing in at eleven pounds, eight ounces. His parents named him Leslie Alexander, straying from the Scottish naming tradition for his first name but did give him his paternal grandfather's name, Alexander, as his middle name.

Childbirth in 1922 was not much different for Jeanie than it had been for her mother in the 1890s. The majority (ninety-five percent) of Scottish women still utilized a midwife to assist them give birth at home. Despite the fact that a Scottish physician had developed anesthetics for childbirth in the previous century, most Scottish women were still giving birth in their homes without the use of anesthesia or other pain killers. Sir James Simpson, a Scottish physician, was a pioneer of obstetrics, gynecology, and childbirth anesthetics. He was the first British physician to use chloroform and ether as anesthetics during childbirth. At the time, Sir James' methods were controversial because many believed the pain of childbirth had been decreed by God as the curse of Eve. His victory was assured when, as personal surgeon to Queen Victoria, he provided her with an anesthetic during the delivery of her seventh child in 1853.[162] Until the advent of the National Health System in the United Kingdom in the 1940s, when childbirth more and more came under the auspices of medical professionals, most working and middle class women continued to give birth at home without the advantage of chloroform or forceps.

Jeanie most likely breastfed her infant. At that time, breastfeeding was believed to make for healthier babies and had the added benefit of being perceived as a natural form of contraception. Most mothers in the working class neighborhoods of Scotland prior to World War II breastfed their infants for the first year of life. It was more economical than expensive infant formula manufactured by companies like Nestle. And more hygienic because sterilizing formula in a kitchen without hot water would have been challenging.

Leslie Alexander was baptized at four weeks of age on September 17, 1922 in St. Kenneth's Linthouse Church by Reverend Samuel Knox, the same minister who had married his parents. St. Kenneth's was just across the street from James and Jeanie Simpson's apartment in Govan. In 1922, St. Kenneth's was associated with the United Free Church of Scotland.

St. Kenneth's Linthouse Church in Govan as it appeared in 1995

The Presbyterian Church, or The Kirk, as it is sometimes called in Scotland, has been the national church of the country since the Scottish Reformation in 1560. Since the time of its formation, many small sects broke away from 'The Kirk' over doctrinal issues. The United Free Church of Scotland was one of those sects that broke away from the larger Presbyterian Church of Scotland for a number of years at the turn of the twentieth century. Today, St. Kenneth's Linthouse Church is a congregation of the Church of Scotland.[163]

The young Simpson couple were living in their small Glasgow tenement when their baby was born, within a short distance of both of their parents.

Jeanie Simpson with her son Leslie Alexander circa 1924 in Glasgow

Jeanie was fulfilling the full-time job of mother and housewife while James was working as a pattern maker in one of the shipbuilding industries on the Clyde. Their lives were not unlike other young married working class couples in Glasgow in the years following the end of World War I. Jeanie's role of housewife was not much easier than it had been for her mother thirty years before. She would have depended on her coal-stoked kitchen range to cook meals for her family and warm her small apartment. She may have had electricity for lamps but these were used sparingly. Jeanie and James still were depending on a shared toilet and their apartment lacked running hot water. Bath time for all three of the Simpsons would have involved heating water on the kitchen range and bathing in a tin tub in the kitchen or taking a 'sponge bath' with a small basin of water heated on the kitchen range. Taking her turn with her fellow neighbors, she would have utilized the wash house in the rear close for her family's laundry. And while her infant, Leslie, was still in diapers (nappies) she would have done his laundry on a daily basis probably in her own kitchen sink, allowing them to dry in the back close or on a wooden rack over the kitchen range if the weather was bad. She shopped on a daily basis from neighborhood shops for fresh produce, meat, fish and dairy products. She took her turn along with her apartment neighbors to keep the entry to her apartment building scrubbed. Scrubbing the landing was done with a bucket of soapy water, a scrub brush and a clean rag (an old towel or undershirt) while on her knees.

Eating out at the neighborhood 'chippie' for a fish and chips meal was an infrequent treat for the Simpsons. But Jeanie was an accomplished cook and baker so eating at home was enjoyable. She excelled at baking and took great pride in her culinary skills. Some of her favorite recipes are included at the end of the book—steak and kidney pie, scones, chicken barley soup, Finnan Haddie, and shortbread. Jeanie, trained as a seamstress, continued to use her skills to sew most of her apparel. She had learned to knit from her mother and enjoyed knitting for herself, her husband and young son.

However, much was happening in Glasgow as the shipbuilding and supporting industries had fallen into a significant downturn after the war. Military orders had come to a sudden halt following the armistice signed on November 11, 1918. Shipyard workers were faced with erratic work schedules or, worse yet, no work at all. All of Clydebank's major employers including the leading John Brown and Company were hit hard with the post-war cessation of naval work. Their quality work in marine engineering and shipbuilding, which had ensured the absolute confidence of two of the world's leading maritime organizations, the Cunard Steamship Company and the Royal Navy meant nothing when the work orders were no longer coming in. During the war years of 1914–1918 the John Brown shipyard had launched forty-five warships. They were responsible for building the *Lusitania* and her sister ship, the *Aquitania*, for the Cunard Line and many other ships that proved to be the epitome of British maritime power. However, the decline in postwar orders could not maintain the workforce on the Clydebank at its wartime levels.

To add to the post wartime woes, worker discontent increased as unemployment levels rose in Scotland to more than fourteen percent in 1923, while it was over eleven percent in the remainder of the United Kingdom.[164] Strikes and protests were led by the socialist Clyde Workers' Committee. Nicknamed 'Red Clydesiders', the strikers were radical socialist trade unionists from the Glasgow engineering factories whose protests culminated in a riot in the city's George Square in 1919, not unlike the socialist revolution in Russia which led to the formation of the Soviet Union. A few years earlier the wives of Glasgow servicemen and munitions workers had conducted a very successful protest when they refused to pay steep rent increases imposed on them by wartime profiteers. Their efforts ended in rents frozen by law.[165]

James Simpson was just completing his apprenticeship as a wooden pattern maker when the post war downturn put his career in jeopardy. Worker unrest and concern over steady employment had to be a concern for James who had a wife and young son to support. Emigration in search of a better life had to be considered.

Scottish emigration was nothing new. Prior to the eighteenth century large numbers of Scots had emigrated to other parts of Europe, including eastern

Europe, Scandinavia, and Ulster (northern Ireland). With the growth of the British colonies in the early 1700s the focus of emigration shifted to British overseas colonies, particularly the English speaking ones including America, Canada, South Africa, Australia and New Zealand. In the 1800s and early 1900s Scotland lost a larger percentage of its population through emigration than any other European country except Ireland and possibly Norway. The trickle of emigrants leaving Scotland became a flood from the middle of the nineteenth century until the third decade of the twentieth century. It is estimated that over two million Scots left their homeland between 1821 and 1915.[166]

The most important factor in the advent of mass emigration was the development of the steam engine. Steamships could cross the Atlantic in a week compared to a sailing ship crossing of six weeks. The rapidly expanding railway networks in Scotland and in North America allowed people to travel easily both to ports of departure and quickly away from ports of arrival. Passenger line steamship companies, along with newspaper advertising and improved communication via postal services and the telegraph, made the process of emigration even easier. Some emigrants from Scotland were tenant farmers or farm servants in search of land. Many others were skilled or semi-skilled urban tradesman like James Simpson. An estimated one-third of those skilled workers who emigrated, did so for short periods of time to take advantage of high wages in other countries, then later returned to Scotland. James' younger brother, Richard Shaw Simpson, was one who emigrated, then returned to Glasgow after several years in the United States.

A famous Scottish emigrant was industrialist Andrew Carnegie[167]. At the age of thirteen, Carnegie emigrated with his parents and younger brother from Scotland in 1848 en route to western Pennsylvania. By 1900 he was the world's richest man after succeeding in the steel industry, a true 'rags to riches' story. In his later years, he turned his energies and his wealth toward philanthropy and is well known both here in the United States as well as his homeland, Scotland, for his generous donations of libraries. Andrew Carnegie believed that public libraries were a good way to socialize immigrants into decent Americans and his philanthropy resulted in the construction of more than twenty-five hundred libraries with almost seventeen hundred of those in the United States. Although he did not donate the monies for the public library in Govan, he was on hand in 1901 to open the Elder Park Library in the Simpson's neighborhood of Govan, within a stone's throw from the Simpson and Russell homes. The Elder Park Library was gifted to the people of Govan by Isabella Elder, widow of marine engineer John Elder. The Russell home was directly across the street from the Elder Park in Govan.

Several United States Presidents were of Scottish descent. Twenty-eighth United States President, Woodrow Wilson, was the grandson of a Scottish

Presbyterian minister. Wilson was born in Staunton, Virginia where his father, Joseph Ruggles Wilson, was also a Presbyterian minister. Other United States presidents of Scots ancestry include William McKinley, Andrew Jackson, Theodore Roosevelt, James Polk, Lyndon B. Johnson, and Ulysses S. Grant.

While contemplating emigration, James Simpson must have been even more concerned when he heard about the change in the United States immigration laws. The United States Immigration Act of 1924, or the Johnson-Reed Act, restricted immigration, reducing the annual quota to only 164,000 immigrants. This was the first permanent limitation on immigration into the United States and established the 'national origins quota system'. Quotas were set for European immigrants so that no more than two percent of the 1890 immigrant stocks were allowed into America. It effectively halted 'undesirable' immigration by imposing quotas based on the country of origin. It was an attempt to preserve the ethnic flavor of the 'old immigrants', those earlier settlers primarily from Northern and Western Europe. The perception existed that the newly arriving immigrants mostly from southern and eastern Europe were somehow inferior to those who arrived earlier. Following 1924, eighty-six percent of immigrants were from Northern European countries with Germany, Britain and Ireland with the highest quotas.[168] It marked the end of mass migration to America and saw the decline of the immigrant processing station at Ellis Island in New York harbor.

After World War I, the United States began to emerge as a potential world power. United States embassies were established in countries all over the world, and prospective immigrants then applied for their visas at American consulates in their countries of origin. The necessary paperwork was completed at the consulate and a medical inspection was also conducted there. After 1924, immigrants to America no longer were required to be processed through Ellis Island.

In 1925, thirty-two year old James Simpson made the momentous and risk-taking decision to leave his job and the familiar and comfortable life he knew in Glasgow to make a new life for himself and his family in the United States. It must have been a wrenching decision to leave behind all that was familiar—his loving and supportive parents, his close-knit family of brothers and sisters (all eleven of them), his cozy apartment in Govan, his familiar neighborhood and friends, and temporarily, at least, his wife and young son who would remain in Glasgow until James had established himself in the United States. For Jeanie, it must have also been a difficult decision to leave her loving parents and siblings to accompany her husband and son to America. Former President John F. Kennedy in his book '*A Nation of Immigrants*' wrote that "little is more extraordinary than the decision to migrate, little more extraordinary than the accumulation of emotions and thoughts which finally leads a family to say farewell to a community where it has lived for centuries, to abandon old ties and familiar landmarks, and to sail across dark seas to a strange land." [169]

The uncertainty of unemployment for a shipbuilding pattern maker in the post World War I years certainly had to be a significant factor in James' decision to emigrate. However, James was also dissatisfied with the 'class distinction' that was so prevalent in Scotland, particularly in the west of Scotland, where Glasgow is located. Later in life he would mention the class distinction that he had perceived as being a major deciding factor for him to emigrate. The United States had a reputation for not being as 'class conscious' as the United Kingdom.

In preparation for his trip, James Simpson would have traveled fifty miles by train to the United States Embassy in Scotland's capitol, Edinburgh, to process a visa in preparation for his travel to America. He would have gone to the Glasgow ticket agency of the Cunard Anchor Line to purchase his ticket. And after bidding farewell to everyone, he boarded the Cunard Anchor Line Steamship *Transylvania III* in November 1925 in the Yorkhill area of Glasgow for the week-long sea journey arriving in New York City on November 16th. Most likely his wife, Jeanie, and young son, Leslie, were at the port as James' ship made its slow departure from its berth in Glasgow on its way across the northern Atlantic Ocean to New York City.

In the early years of the twentieth century, the ocean liner was the primary mode of global transportation and would remain so until the development of commercial airline travel. It was hardly as glamorous as the ocean liner travel that we know today. A number of steamship companies provided trans-Atlantic service from the British Isles to North American ports including the famous White Star Line (owners of the *Titanic*), the Cunard Line (owners of the *Queen Elizabeth* and *Queen Mary*), the Hamburg America Line and the Holland America Line. The Anchor Line's *Transylvania III* was a twin screw, three-funnel, turbine steamship. Interestingly, only one of the funnels was operational, the other two were just for 'looks'. It had been built in the Simpson's backyard at Govan's Fairfield Shipbuilding and Engineering Company's shipyard in 1925 and made its maiden voyage on September 12, 1925, just two months prior to James' boarding. It sailed from Glasgow to New York City with a brief stop to pick up additional Irish passengers in Moville(Londonderry) at the northern tip of Ireland, county Donegal. The *Transylvania III* could transport a total of 1423 passengers, 279 in first class, 344 in second class and 800 in third class.

By 1925, the Glasgow-based Cunard Anchor Line, one of the most popular Atlantic passenger lines, had more than seventy years experience transporting passengers between New York, Londonderry and Glasgow. In 1911

Anchor Line was acquired by its rival company, the British-owned Cunard Line, and operated until 1956 under the name Cunard Anchor Line. The line bragged that it had the 'fastest passenger and freight steamers in the world'. During the winter months the *Transylvania* and its sister ships, the *Caledonia*, the *California*, and the *Cameronia*, were used as cruise ships, primarily in the Mediterranean. The remainder of the year they transported passengers between Glasgow and New York. Many of the passengers on the west bound leg (Glasgow to New York) were emigrants.

Most likely James traveled as a second or third class traveler. Although we don't know what his passenger fare was research has shown that in 1912 a second class ticket from New York to Glasgow was purchased for fifty US dollars. Class divisions aboard the *Transylvania III* mirrored the social structure of the time. Distinctions among first, second and third class were evident in the division of onboard amenities. The ship was a large, floating hotel with a commercial kitchen, laundry and on-board entertainment. It boasted separate dining rooms for its first, second and third class passengers, a first and second class smoking room for the gentlemen, broad decks, a garden lounge, a gymnasium, and an elevator. An army of more than three hundred staff members provided services for passengers and kept the ship running smoothly. Deck life was the most exciting part of the transatlantic voyage. On a pleasant day in good weather conditions, the decks were filled with guests playing shuffleboard and other games. The deck was a place of bracing fresh air, a place to meet fellow passengers and to imagine what the future held.

Undoubtedly James was happy to arrive in America after a weeklong sea journey and get his first view of the Statue of Liberty in New York harbor. At that time, the port at New York harbor was the most popular destination for emigrant ships from Europe. Other destination ports included Boston, Philadelphia, Baltimore, Charleston, New Orleans, and several Canadian ports. Lady Liberty was often one of the first glimpses of the United States millions of immigrants viewed after their long sea journey from Europe. Ships from Europe passed from the Atlantic Ocean through the Verrazano Narrows, the gateway of America, into the harbor where Bedloe's Island stands with Lady Liberty. A gift from the people of France, the statue was erected in New York harbor in 1886 so that by the time James arrived the Statue had been looking out over the harbor for almost forty years. Since that time it has become one of the most recognizable symbols of the United States.

Upon arrival in New York City, the *Transylvania III* would have docked at the Hudson or East River piers where James and his fellow passengers would have disembarked and presented their passports or visas to the U.S. Customs officer. James would have found the exchange bureau where he would have changed his Scottish pounds into United States dollars, a telegraph office where he could have sent a telegram to Glasgow informing his Scottish loved ones of his safe arrival in New York, and he could have purchased a rail ticket for the second leg of his trip from New York to Chicago.

We do not know why James chose to settle in the Chicago, Illinois area when he emigrated to the United States. We don't know whether he had the promise of a job in Chicago to come to or whether he chose to settle in Chicago, then found employment. But we do know that once he settled in Chicago he made friends with two other young Scots, Alec Davis and Peter Souter, who also settled in the Chicago area with their families. Since Alec (probably Alexander) Davis had arrived in the United States in 1923 and heralded from Glasgow, it is possible that he alerted James Simpson to the possibility of employment in the Chicago area.

Once James arrived in Chicago he found temporary housing by renting a room in the home of Mrs. Carlson at 3533 West Adams Street, a short half mile distance from his work at Crane Valve Company. This was probably a boarding house-type arrangement where Mrs. Carlson provided a room and his meals. He could have walked to work or taken public transportation. Automobiles were in use in Chicago but James could not afford a car at that time. Although the automobile made expansion into the Chicago suburbs possible in the 1920s as more and more people purchased their own car, only one in every eight Chicagoans owned their own automobile. By 1930, Chicago lagged behind state and national averages when one in every five persons were car owners. [170] And even though Henry Ford's Model T automobile made car ownership within reach of the working and middle class, most Chicagoans were slow to change their transportation habits.

James depended on public transportation in Chicago as he had in Glasgow. The Chicago Rapid Transit Company, formed in 1924 from four smaller elevated railroad operators all dating from the 1890s, provided transportation for many city residents via electric trolleys during the first part of the twentieth century. In 1947, the transit company would become known as the Chicago Transit Authority and still provides transportation today for many Chicago residents.

James, like other immigrants from the British Isles, was able to quickly blend into the dominant Anglo-American culture. To his American neighbors and co-workers, he hardly seemed like a foreigner. His vocational training allowed him to excel in his new employment. He spoke their language (although with a soft Scottish burr) and attended their Protestant church. His attire was very similar to theirs. We know that he did seek out fellow Scots as friends but quickly made American friends, as well.

It must have been a long eleven months before his wife, Jeanie, and son, Leslie, could join him in Chicago. From immigration records we know that his friend Peter Souter and Peter's wife Margaret Jane (nicknamed Maggie), both natives of Lossiemouth, Scotland did not arrive in Chicago until August 1927. Glasgow draftsman and friend, Alec Davis, had arrived two years earlier and possibly was also employed at the Crane Valve Company.

In the 1920s, Chicago was a major industrial and manufacturing city. James found employment as a pattern maker with the Crane Valve Company at their manufacturing facility in Chicago on South Kedzie Avenue, just west of the downtown area. During the 1920s, when Crane expanded overseas, the company was the world's leading manufacturer of valves and fittings. The company supplied much of the pipe used for the large central heating systems in Chicago's new skyscrapers, and it was also selling the enameled cast-iron products that were soon found in bathrooms and kitchens in residences across the country. In the 1940s when America went to war, the Crane Company supported the war effort by manufacturing valves for ships, something very familiar to pattern maker James. Crane supplied the United States Navy, the Atomic Energy Commission, and new manufacturers of high-octane fuel using catalytic cracking techniques. At the time James Simpson worked for Crane the company employed about five thousand workers and had expanded its operations internationally into Canada, England and France.[171]

Once in the United States, James worked and saved, planning to have his family join him in Chicago as soon as possible. And that was accomplished the following year in October, 1926. Jeanie and four year old Leslie boarded another Cunard Anchor Line ship, the *Cameronia II,* and disembarked in New York on October 23, 1926 where her husband James met her. It must have been difficult for the elder Russells, Adam and Helen, to say farewell to their daughter, Jeanie, and grandson Leslie, knowing that they might never see them again. Prior to the advent of airline travel, only the wealthy had sufficient funds to allow them to travel 'across the pond' on an ocean liner. Emigrants would save up until they could afford the one-way fare but usually knew that they would not be able to return home due to the expenses involved in ocean travel.

The Western Union telegram that was sent by Jeanie to James from Glasgow, dated October 18, 1926 and delivered to James from the Western Union office in Chicago announced their arrival in New York on October 23, 1926. Aboard ship Jeanie had her hands full with a curious and precocious four year old. During her later years, she told her daughter-in-law Virginia how she had to watch her rambunctious little boy very carefully especially when they were on deck because little Leslie wanted to climb the deck rails. Luckily his mother was able to control him and succeeded in keeping him from falling overboard!

The *Cameronia II* was a sister ship to the *Transylvania III* which eleven months previously had brought James to New York. Built by another Glasgow shipbuilding firm, William Beardmore and Company, the *Cameronia II* was launched in 1919 but did not make its maiden voyage until May 11, 1921, her outfitting delayed by a strike. Beardmore, was a Scottish engineering and shipbuilding company based in Glasgow and the surrounding Clydeside area. It was active between about 1890 and 1930 and at its peak employed about forty thousand workers. The *Cameronia II* was slightly larger and could accommodate a total of 1726 passengers, 256 in first class, 370 in second class, and 1100 in third class. A crew of 320 cared for the passengers. It is likely that Jeanie and Leslie traveled in second or third class.

Two years later, James' brother, Richard Shaw Simpson, emigrated and joined James' family in Chicago. Richard, two years younger than James, was a machinist. He sailed from Glasgow, Scotland in May 1927 aboard the steam ship *Montclare* (another Glasgow built ship built at the shipyards of the John Brown Company) which sailed from Glasgow to Quebec, Canada. From Canada, Richard made his way to Chicago, probably by rail. In the 1930 United States census was living with his brother James, his wife Jeanie and their son Leslie. Richard probably came to Chicago through a Canadian port because of the recent United States immigration laws (the Immigration Act of 1924) which limited immigration from the United Kingdom to less than 68,000 per year. It was a common practice to emigrate to Canada and subsequently cross the border, often illegally, in an effort to circumvent American quota regulations. [172] Richard would not stay long in the United States. He left and returned to Glasgow in the early 1930s. While employed in the United States he worked as an automobile mechanic in a car factory in the Chicago area.

When the Simpsons arrived in the United States, Calvin Coolidge was the U.S. President, the Volstead Act of 1920 (Prohibition) making the sale of alcohol unlawful was still in effect, American women had earned the right to vote in national elections several years previously (1919), and Chicago was making history as the home of notorious gangsters like Al Capone, Americans could purchase a Model T Ford for $290, flappers were dancing the *Charleston* and the song *Chicago, That Toddling Town* became popular.

The reunited Simpson family was ready to start their new lives together in America.

Chapter 10

Simpson Couple—The Middle Years

Scottish immigrants, James and Jeanie Simpson, along with their young son, Leslie, were on their way to becoming Americans. We do not know where the family first called home when Jeanie and young Leslie first arrived and joined James in Chicago. But, by the time the 1930 United States federal census was compiled, James and Jeanie along with their 7 ½ year old son Leslie, as well as James' brother, Richard Simpson, were renting a house (at sixty-five dollars per month rent) in Brookfield Village at 232 North Blanchan Avenue. Brookfield Village, a Chicago suburb located thirteen miles west of downtown, is the location of Chicago's world famous zoo, Brookfield Zoo. The family would later move to Huron Street in the Austin area of Chicago, just two blocks north of the Crisler home on Race Avenue.

In the spring of 1929 Jeanie applied for immigration visas for herself and her son in order to return to Glasgow to visit her family. The Washington, D.C. office of the United States Immigration and Naturalization Service awarded these visas in June 1929 and travel plans were made for Jeanie and Leslie to make the sea journey back to Glasgow in the late summer of 1929. It was the only time she would be able to make this trip and it is not known whether or not there was a special reason for this trip. Could there have been an ill parent or sibling or even the death of a family member? This is an area for further research.

At some point during their stay in Scotland, Jeanie and Leslie travelled to the sea coast west of Glasgow. James' youngest sister, Elizabeth Simpson McColl, lived there in the same coastal town of Largs where she was the proud proprietor of an exclusive women's clothing store, McColl's. A short ferry ride from Largs, across the harbor in the Firth of Clyde, is the resort town of Millport. Glaswegians often visited Largs and Millport during the summer months for a 'wee' outing. A photo of young Leslie captures his delight in the cold waters of the North Sea.

*Leslie Simpson at Millport beach on west coast of
Scotland August 1929*

One of the memorable stories from that trip that would be recounted for many years within the family was the tonsillectomy story. During their stay in Glasgow seven year old Leslie developed a bad case of tonsillitis and it was decided that a tonsillectomy was the best plan of action, the sooner, the better. A Scottish physician came to the Russell home and Leslie had his tonsils removed while lying on the kitchen table in the home of his grandparents in Govan. Following his recovery, Jeanie and Leslie returned home aboard the Cunard Anchor Line steamship, the *California*, arriving in New York on September 23, 1929, then made their way by train home to Chicago.

Prior to the onset of the Great Depression in 1929 the family's fortunes must have been looking up for the Simpsons. The family's finances were sufficient to allow Jeanie and young Leslie to plan a several week visit home to

Glasgow. They were establishing themselves in their new country. James had a good job with a stable company and was making a very good wage as a pattern maker for the Crane Valve Company. Jeanie was adjusting to her new American life as a mother and housewife in Chicago. Their only child, Leslie, had started kindergarten at age five in the Chicago public school system.

School photo circa 1928 Leslie Simpson is in second row,
first boy on left

We don't know for sure which Chicago school Leslie attended but his wife, Virginia, thinks that he attended the Hayes Elementary School in the Austin area of Chicago at least for a portion of his elementary school years. Hayes School was the same school that Virginia's younger sister, Emily attended after the Crislers moved from Waukegan to Chicago. The Simpson couple was renting a house and both still depended on public transportation to get to work, to shop and to go to church.

The Great Depression was particularly severe in Chicago, the largest manufacturing city in the country at the time. Because of the city's reliance on manufacturing, the hardest hit sector nationally, Chicago suffered more than some others during the Depression years. Only fifty percent of the Chicagoans who had worked in the manufacturing sector in 1927 were still working there in 1933.[173] Luckily, James was one of those who maintained his employment throughout the 1930s. He was fortunate that he had chosen employment with the Crane Company. Although the company in 1931 reported its first operating loss in the company's history, as the decade continued it was able to recover. By 1934, Crane was able to offer shares on the New York Stock Exchange. It sustained its growth through the latter years of the Depression and was well poised to supply the needs of the United States Navy as the United States entered World War II.

We have no specific knowledge of how difficult or easy the transition was for the Simpsons as they assimilated into the American scene. In their later years they seldom spoke of their early years as immigrants in the Chicago area, or in fact, their early years in Glasgow. Despite the tribulations of the Depression years experienced by all Americans, the family prospered. We do know that James and Jeanie enjoyed a radio in their home and listened to programs like George Burns and Gracie Allen as well as Jack Benny and Fibber McGee and Molly. Their only son adjusted to life in Chicago and had very little memory of his life in the Glasgow tenements. Although during the Depression years it was sometimes difficult to obtain all of the necessary ingredients, Jeanie enjoyed preparing her Scottish recipes in her modern kitchen. She surely appreciated the hot water supplied to her kitchen and bathroom, electrical lighting both inside and outside her home, the central heating in their rental house, and the ice box which allowed her to store food items negating the need to shop for food supplies daily.

The Simpsons had just one child. Leslie would not have the advantage of having a little brother or sister and we do not know whether or not this was intentional or not. Prior to the development and availability of birth control pills one has to wonder how they were able to not have additional children unless there were infertility issues. Literature describing sex education provided to young Scots girls in the early 1900s indicates that it was practically non-existent. Many young women were totally unknowledgeable about 'the birds and the bees' and went to their wedding totally innocent of the expectations ahead. One young Scotswoman of that era stated that 'you had your family after you were married because you did not know how not to have a family'.[174] One of my memories of my Simpson grandparents may lend a clue to this question. When I was four and five years old we lived with them in the Chicago suburb of Elmwood Park in an upstairs apartment. There, my parents, my brothers, Jim and Paul, and I lived upstairs while our Simpson grandparents lived downstairs. My grandparents, at that time, had separate bedrooms and my mother remembers that for as long as she knew them, they did not share the same bedroom. So, it is possible that abstinence was how they prevented further pregnancies.

The Simpsons were church-goers and joined the Methodist Church in the Austin area of Chicago while they were living on Huron Street, just a few blocks distant. Jeanie involved herself in the women's groups at the church.

Their son, Leslie, attended church and Sunday School and during his high school years attended the Sunday evening youth meetings called the Epworth League. Other members of the Epworth League at Austin Methodist Church included his future wife, Virginia Crisler, as well as later famous Hugh Hefner. As an adult, Hefner became world famous as a business man and editor of the Playboy magazine.

Sometime in 1939 or 1940 James became the proud owner of his first automobile, a dark green Buick four-door sedan. After a lifetime of depending on public transportation to get to work, both in Glasgow and now in Chicago, he finally had the freedom afforded by an automobile that he could park outside his own home. Jeanie, however, would never learn to drive a car and depended on James or her son, Leslie, to drive her.

Son Leslie graduated from Chicago's Austin High School in June 1941.

Leslie Simpson-Austin High School graduation photo 1940

At that time, Europe had been at war for almost two years following the invasion of Poland by Adolf Hitler's German troops in September 1939. Americans across the country, including the Simpsons, were all holding their breath in anticipation of America becoming involved in this conflict. James and Jeanie were justifiably concerned knowing that their only son could be sent off to war. He was a young healthy male and a prime candidate for the military draft as the United States geared up for the possibility of going to war. They encouraged their son to enlist in the navy rather than be drafted into the army. This advice was probably based, at least partially, on their Scottish families' long association with the sea in the shipbuilding and the fishing industries.

Meanwhile, Leslie found employment following high school graduation with the Pennsylvania Railroad. He started out as a fireman in the railroad yards in Chicago and quickly moved up to the position of messenger, taking messages between Union Station in Chicago and the downtown Pennsylvania Railroad Chicago offices. The Pennsylvania Railroad, commonly referred to as the Pennsy, was headquartered in Philadelphia and had a mainline between Philadelphia and Chicago. The Pennsy, or PRR, founded in 1846, was the largest railroad by traffic and revenue in the United States throughout the twentieth century. At one time the Pennsy was the largest publicly traded corporation in the world.[175]

Shortly afterwards, Leslie made his decision about enlistment and joined the United States Naval Reserve. He trained for eight weeks at Great Lakes Training Center located in North Chicago. Located between the affluent North Shore area of Chicago and the industrialized area of Waukegan, Great Lakes was not far from his parents home. Except for the time that Les was involved in his naval reserve training, he would continue to live at home with his parents until he married in 1943. During World War II, the training center at Great Lakes supplied more than one million trained sailors for the war effort. Interestingly, Great Lakes, the largest single training facility for the U.S. Navy, is a thousand miles from the nearest ocean. It did, however, have the advantage of being close to Chicago's rail hub and the major population center of one of the largest Midwestern cities. During World War II, Great Lakes was one of the Navy's most important centers for both basic and advanced training. While there the recruits had reveille at 5:30 A.M., field days on Fridays and barracks inspections on Saturdays. Seamen stood duty every four days and had liberty from Saturdays at noon until 7:30 A.M. Mondays. After a basic four-week course, students went on to advanced training in various areas including radioman, quartermaster and signalman or yeomen and storekeeper. During wartime, the average student population at Great Lakes was 5,500 and a seaman earned $1,700 a year.[176] Following completion of his basic training. Leslie went on to training at gunnery school in Memphis, Tennessee. While in the navy he would serve as an aviation machinist mate, repairing aircraft engines.

As her only son was preparing for his high school graduation Jeanie Simpson was preparing for her naturalization ceremony. She had made the decision to become a United States citizen. The naturalization process is a three part process and normally takes approximately five years to complete. After living in the United States for two years and desiring to become a citizen, Jeanie would have filed a record of her intent to become a naturalized citizen, referred to as the 'first papers'. After another two years, she would have petitioned for naturalization, known as the 'final papers'. On March 27, 1941 her request for citizenship was granted and her papers were issued by the United States District Court of the Northern District of Illinois in Chicago, the third and final part. No record of James Simpson's naturalization has been located. It is possible that Jeanie became a citizen so that her son would automatically become a citizen once her papers were granted. And indeed, son Leslie requested his mother's naturalization papers on several occasions to prove his citizenship, particularly when he enlisted in the Navy Reserve and when he went to work for the railroad. James may have maintained his British citizenship so that the family had one foot in each country. In addition, during World War II aliens were required to register their presence in the country through the Alien Registration Program. However, attempts to locate these records of James Simpson registering as an alien have proved futile as well.

In April 1943, twenty year old seaman Les started dating a former high school schoolmate with whom he had become reacquainted with while participating in Austin Methodist Church's Epworth League activities, Virginia Crisler. The young couple would meet after work and double-date with another young sailor couple, Harry and Marian Carle. Harry was a sailor as well and Marion worked with Virginia at Buick Motors as an airplane engine tester. By August 1943, Les and Virginia had decided to marry and both sets of parents were aware of their plans to marry in December 1943. Days later, however, Les received orders to report for sea duty. Les and Virginia made the decision to elope and convinced their minister to marry them in the church parsonage on August 7, 1943 prior to Les shipping out. Both bride and groom were only twenty years old. Les would not be twenty-one until August 19th. Not being twenty-one and not wanting to have to get his parent's permission to marry, Les was able to convince a fellow sailor yeoman to change the age on his identification card so that they could obtain a marriage license without his parent's permission. Virginia informed her mother and got her written permission to marry. Harry and Marion Carle acted as their best man and matron of honor. They spent their one-night honeymoon in a small hotel in downtown Chicago.

Nine days later Les shipped out en route to Norfolk, Virginia headed for the destroyer *USS Fogg*. Jeanie and her new daughter-in-law, Virginia, accompanied Les to Union Station in Chicago to see him off and wish him well. The *USS Fogg*, a destroyer escort, had just been commissioned in July 1943 and was headed out to sea with its complement of two hundred sailors and officers for its shakedown cruise in the Atlantic Ocean. Working up and down the east coast of the United States the *Fogg* worked with a submarine so that the crew of the *Fogg* could familiarize themselves with conditions under fire. The submarine towed a target while the *Fogg's* seamen would fire at the target and put depth charges over the side of the ship just as though the target was an enemy submarine.

Out to sea for only one month, Les developed severe back pain which was later diagnosed as a fractured vertebra in his lower back. He was taken off the *Fogg* and transported to Chelsea Naval Hospital outside of Boston, Massachusetts where he was hospitalized for treatment. It was determined that he had been injured weeks earlier while at Glenview Air Station outside of Chicago when the Navy plane he was aboard made a crash landing. As the plane was landing a large gust of wind caught it and flipped it over. Les and his fellow crew members were initially relieved believing that they had only suffered bumps and bruises. Les would later find out he had been injured more seriously.

Following notification by the Navy, his wife Virginia joined him in Chelsea and got a rented room in nearby Boston where she could visit her new husband regularly. Les would remain hospitalized through the end of December 1943. At that time he was discharged from the hospital. He would return to the hospital on a daily basis for out-patient treatment until March 1944 when he was medically discharged from treatment and honorably discharged from the Navy. Both Les and Virginia were pleased and excited to return home to parents and extended family in Chicago arriving the day before Virginia's twenty-second birthday, March 20, 1944.

Meanwhile, at home, his parents continued to support the war effort. During the months that their son was serving in the Navy the Simpsons hung a small 'Son in Service' flag in their front window. These flags consisted of a blue star in the center of the red-bordered white rectangle signifying that a family member was in active service. The star was replaced (or covered) with a gold star if the family member died in action.

James' job at Crane directly supported the war effort through supplying the needs of the Navy with valves for ships. At home, James did not have to worry about the rationing of automobile tires and gasoline since he was not a car owner at the time and he and Jeanie still depended on public transportation. Jeanie, like millions of other American women, donated hand-knit scarves and socks for servicemen through her volunteer work at her church. She did her share in recycling commodities that were vital to the war effort including tin, aluminum, rubber, waste kitchen fats, glass, and paper. Jeanie's shopping and food preparation habits were severely impacted by the shortages of wartime. Like other Americans, the Simpsons had to contend with the wartime rationing on products like sugar, coffee, tea, cheese, butter, margarine, meat, lard and many others. Jeanie practiced frugality by sewing and repairing her own clothes with her excellent dressmaking skills learned years earlier in Glasgow.

James and Jeanie Simpson outside their
Chicago home circa 1943

James and Jeanie were undoubtedly concerned about their families back home in Glasgow when the Clydebank came under attack during the early years of the war. In March 1941, German Luftwaffe air raids practically destroyed the town of Clydebank. Wanting to destroy the United Kingdom's ability to produce naval ships and munitions, Clydebank suffered significant damages. It's citizens were affected as well with more than five hundred civilian deaths and more than 600 severely injured. Of the twelve thousand homes in Clydebank, only seven remained undamaged following the bombings.[177]

The Simpsons were very pleased when they learned that their son and his wife would be returning home in March, 1944. Initially, the young couple had difficulty finding an apartment and moved in with his parents. Les returned to his job at the Pennsylvania Railroad and wife Virginia was hired by the PRR in their payroll department as a comptometer operator.

The Simpsons would become first time grandparents when their son and daughter-in-law informed them that Virginia was expecting their first grandchild in late 1944. James Russell Simpson was born in Chicago on March 30, 1945. Named according to Scottish tradition after his paternal grandfather. James. And his middle name was from his paternal grandmother's maiden name, James Russell. Jimmie, as he soon became to the family, not to be confused with his grandfather James, became the 'apple' of his grandmother's eye.

Jeanie Simpson with first grandson, James Russell
Simpson circa 1946

A momentous day for the Simpsons occurred in 1951 when the Scottish immigrants became proud owners of their first home. Since their arrival in the United States in the mid 1920s the Simpsons had lived in rental properties. They purchased a small two story brick house in the Chicago suburb of Elmwood Park.

Simpson home in Elmwood Park, Illinois circa 1950

Son and daughter-in-law, Virginia and their children would also move into this home in a two bedroom upstairs apartment. Jeanie enjoyed having her grandchildren, little Jimmie, Leslie Ann, and toddler Paul close by so that she could see them daily.

Simpson family dinner in Elmwood Park. Jeanie, Leslie, Virginia, Jimmy and Leslie Ann circa 1948

Simpson family at Brookfield Zoo circa 1948

However, her happiness was short lived. In late 1952 Jeanie became ill and was diagnosed with lymphoma, a form of cancer of the lymphatic system. Lymphoma is a cancer that develops more often in older individuals and the risk increases with age. The average age at diagnosis is in the 60s. It is more common in men and less common in people of African American and Asian American descent. Jeanie was fifty eight years old at diagnosis. She lost her courageous battle on November 17, 1953 while hospitalized in the same Chicago hospital where her grandchildren were born, West Suburban Hospital. With help from his son's father-in-law, Orval Crisler, James Simpson purchased a burial plot in the Acacia Park cemetery in Chicago. Acacia Park, located on Irving Park Boulevard, is associated with the Masonic organization and Orval was able to assist James purchase two burials plots there, one for Jeanie and one for himself at Acacia Park.

Chapter 11
James Simpson—The Later Years

James was now a widower but not alone since his son's family lived upstairs in his Elmwood Park home. He continued to work at Crane Company and would do so until he retired following a full career as a wooden pattern maker. But change was just around the corner for the entire Simpson family, father and son. As post World War II housing was catching up with the post war housing demand the younger Simpson family made the move in early 1954 to the Chicago suburb of Wheaton, twenty-five miles west of the city. The small upstairs two bedroom apartment had become crowded with the arrival of third child, Paul, in 1951 and the young Simpson family needed more space for their growing family. Wheaton was an ideal choice since it was only two miles from Virginia's parents, Orval and Jennie Crisler, who had settled in the neighboring town of Glen Ellyn a few years earlier. James sold the home he had shared with Jeanie in Elmwood Park while son Les and daughter-in-law Virginia purchased a brand new ranch-style home with one bathroom, three bedrooms and an enclosed back porch that was transformed into an additional bedroom. An attached one car garage was typical for the suburban houses being built in the early 1950s in the Midwest. A small yard of approximately one quarter of an acre was larger than the family had ever had. There was ample space for everyone. A bedroom for grandfather James, one for parents Les and Virginia, one for the two small boys, Jim and Paul, to share and one for Leslie Ann. The two eldest grandchildren, Jim and Leslie Ann, transferred from Elmwood Park Elementary School to the neighborhood Wheaton school, Hawthorne Elementary School, a few blocks away from their home on Wakeman Avenue.

The 1950s brought many technological changes including the new invention, television. Called "one of the most far-reaching changes in communications worldwide"[178]the television soon became the dominant mass media. Television broadcasting had started in 1939 but it's development was delayed during the years of the early 1940s when the world was preoccupied with the war. In the early 1950s television really 'took off' and became a major social force impacting the American family in many ways. Families no longer gathered at the dinner table to discuss the day's events but ate their TV dinners on TV trays in front of the small black and white television set in their living room. The elder Simpsons (James and Jeanie) purchased their first black and white television set while they lived in Elmwood Park in the early 1950s. In 1954 an 'Admiral' brand television set could be purchased for about three hundred dollars, not an inexpensive expenditure for a family. Compare that to the cost of a new 1954 Chevrolet sedan which cost nineteen hundred dollars.[179]

James particularly enjoyed watching sporting events on television, especially the 'fights'. After a long work week, Friday evenings would find James in his bedroom, cigar in hand, with his television tuned to the *Gillette Cavalcade of Sports*, especially if boxing was on the program. Many well-known boxers were featured on this show in the 1950s including Rocky Marciano and Sugar Ray Robinson.

Shortly following James' move to the suburban town of Wheaton he made his one trip back to Glasgow, Scotland to visit his family. Since emigrating to the United States in 1925 James had never made the transatlantic trip despite the fact that Jeanie and Leslie had made the trip in 1929. Rather than travel by steamship James flew from Chicago to Glasgow, Scotland via Pan American Airlines aboard a Douglas DC-6. The DC-6 was considered to be the best airplane in its class when it was built in the late 1940s and early 1950s. It could accommodate between 54 and 102 passengers with three crew members. It was the first Douglas model made with a pressurized cabin.[180] The overnight flight to Europe aboard the DC-6 was certainly much faster than his sea journey aboard the *SS Transylvania* thirty years earlier. While in Glasgow he visited with his many brothers and sisters and their families. It must have been quite a reunion for the Simpson clan! Arriving home after his two week trip he brought gifts for his grandchildren including beautiful engraved silver napkin rings and wool school blazers, red for Leslie Ann and navy blue for Paul and Jimmie. He encouraged two of his sisters, Mary and youngest sister, Elizabeth, to make the trip from Glasgow to Chicago the following summer to visit with him and his son's family in Wheaton. They were the only family members of either James or Jeanie to ever make the trip to America to visit.

The mid 1950s would bring more changes to James' family when his only son, Les, Virginia and their children moved from Wheaton to the Philadelphia suburbs. Les was transferred to a new position in the Pennsylvania Railroad's headquarters in downtown Philadelphia. In preparation for the move, Les and Virginia sold their home in Wheaton. James, who planned to remain in Illinois, purchased a new home for himself in Wheaton.

James would not be alone for long following his son's departure for Pennsylvania. He met and married Lillian Berndtson shortly after Les and his family had moved to Pennsylvania. Lillian, age fifty one, was a single woman, twelve years younger than James when they married on December 28, 1957. She had worked as a bookkeeper in a bank prior to her marriage. Her family was of Swedish descent and she had emigrated to the United States settling in the Chicago area with her parents and other siblings when she was only two years old. James and Lillian would enjoy a twenty year marriage before James' death.

James Simpson circa 1971

James continued to work at the Crane Company until his retirement at age 65. In June, 1966 following his retirement, he and Lillian chose to move to Sister Bay, Wisconsin. There they purchased a small bungalow-style home outside the small (less than one thousand inhabitants) village of Sister Bay. Located along the shore of Lake Michigan in sparsely populated Door County, Sister Bay was established by Norwegian immigrants in the early part of the twentieth century. It had a strong Scandinavian heritage. Door County is a narrow 'thumb' of land that projects out into Lake Michigan and is surrounded on three sides by water. Today as it was in the 1960s and 1970s Door County is a popular tourist and vacation destination.

James and Lillian Simpson holding great grandson David Fetterman June 1972

James, Leslie, Roger and David Fetterman outside the Simpson's Sister Bay home in 1972

James and Lillian enjoyed ten quiet years of retirement together in their Sister Bay home. They became contributing members of the community and were involved in their church, First Baptist Church of Sister Bay, and several other social organizations. In August 1968 they travelled by plane to Pennsylvania for their granddaughter's marriage when Leslie Ann married Roger Louis Fetterman. During several holiday seasons James found employment at a nearby retail establishment as their Santa Claus. Several of the parents commented that they were surprised by Santa's Scottish burr in the Midwestern state of Wisconsin. Despite having immigrated more than forty years prior James still sported a significant, charming Scottish accent. He was a soft-spoken man who was undoubtedly a warm and wonderful Santa.

In mid 1976 James was hospitalized in St. Mary's Hospital in nearby Green Bay, Wisconsin with a heart attack and died on June 6, 1976 at age eighty-three. His obituary which appeared in the local Sister Bay newspaper read as follows:

> *James Simpson, 83, died Sunday, June 6 at St. Mary's Hospital, Green Bay. He was born on May 20, 1893 in Glasgow Scotland to Alexander and Mary Simpson*
>
> *He moved to Sister Bay from Wheaton, Illinois in June, 1966. He was a pattern maker before his retirement. Simpson was a member of the First Baptist church of Sister Bay, the Nor-Dor Senior Citizens, and was active in the Scand organization.*
>
> *On December 28, 1957, he married Lillian Berndtson of Chicago, Illinois. She survives him as well as one son, Leslie A. Simpson, Berwyn, PA; four sisters living in Scotland; three grandchildren and three great-grandchildren.*
>
> *Funeral services will be conducted by the Rev. Lester Weko at the First Baptist Church at 2 PM Wednesday, June 9th with interment in the Little Sister cemetery. Friends may call at the Caspers funeral home, Sister Bay from 4 to 9 PM Tuesday and until noon on Wednesday and then at the church from 1 PM until the time of the service. "*

Lillian would out-live her husband by another twenty-eight years. She died in a Door County nursing home at age 98 in January 2004. Lillian and James Simpson are buried side-by-side in Little Sister Cemetery in Sister Bay, Wisconsin.

Chapter 12

Conclusion

So who were these four people? They were quiet, affectionate people who had a deep appreciation for the importance of family in their lives, a strong work ethic, and a deep spiritual faith. In quiet unassuming ways they proved that they indeed were risk takers for their families in order to provide better lives for themselves and their children. All were born in the latter part of the nineteenth century. They were witnesses to an amazing variety of technological advances which they wholeheartedly embraced.

My memory of them is of loving grandparents who took great pleasure in their children and grandchildren. Their love will remain a cherished memory to me. I am hopeful that this book will allow their sense of family to be passed on to my children, grandchildren and generations to come.

Family Recipes

Chicken Barley Soup
Jeanie Thomson Simpson
Adapted by Leslie Simpson Hall

1 cup finely chopped onion
1 cup chopped carrot
½ cup chopped celery
2 garlic cloves, finely minced
2 teaspoons butter
2 (14 1/2) oz) cans low sodium chicken broth
1 ¾ cups water
¼ teaspoon salt
¼ teaspoon dried thyme
¼ teaspoon black pepper
1 cup chopped cooked chicken
½ cup uncooked quick-cooking barley

Sauté first 4 ingredients in butter in a large Dutch oven over medium heat 5 minutes or until transparent. Add chicken broth, 1 ¾ cups water, and next 3 ingredients. Bring to a boil, reduce heat, and simmer, partially covered about 25 minutes or until vegetables are tender. Add chicken and barley; cook an additional 8 to 10 minutes or until barley is tender.

Steak and Kidney Pie
Jeanie Thomson Simpson

1 lb. beef round steak
1 beef kidney
1/4 cup all-purpose flour
1 teaspoon salt
1/8 teaspoon pepper
3 tablespoon lard or drippings
1 medium sized onion, chopped
2 tablespoon Worcestershire sauce
1/4 teaspoon thyme
1 1/2 cup water
Pastry for 1 crust pie

Cut round steak in 3/4 to 1 inch cubes. Remove tubes and fat from kidney and cut in 3/4 to 1 inch cubes. Combine flour, salt and pepper. Dredge steak and kidney cubes in seasoned flour (reserving any extra flour) and brown in lard or drippings. Remove meat from frying pan. Add onion to drippings and cook over low heat until transparent. Pour off drippings, add Worcestershire sauce, thyme and water to onion in frying pan and bring to boil. Stir in browned meat cubes and any remaining seasoned flour. Invert 9 inch pie plate over pastry rolled to about 1/8 inch thickness. Cut a circle about an inch from rim of plate for top crust. Cut a design in crust to allow steam to escape.

Cut a second circle about 3/4 to 1 inch from edge of top crust to provide pastry to circle edge of pie plate. Moisten edge of plate and top with outer circle of pastry, adjusting to fit. Turn meat mixture into pie plate and cover with top crust. Seal top pastry to edge and flute. Bake in preheated 325 degree oven for 1 1/2 hours. Makes 6 servings.

Scottish Scones
Jeanie Thomson Simpson
Thanks to Virginia Crisler Simpson

2 cups all purpose flour
4 teaspoons sugar
4 teaspoons baking powder
½ cup (1 stick) butter or margarine

½ teaspoon salt

1 egg—well beaten into whole milk to measure ¾ cup

To softened butter or margarine, add dry ingredients and using a pastry blender work in until well blended. Make a well in flour mixture and add liquid. Mix together until dough forms a ball. Transfer ball onto a lightly floured surface and knead lightly 3-4 times. Pat dough to about ¾ - 1" thick. Cut with round biscuit cutter or with knife into squares. Place on ungreased baking sheet. Bake at 425 º on bottom rack for 5 minutes. Move to top rack and bake until very lightly browned around edges. Best eaten when warm with butter and orange marmalade.

I often use scones as a basis for shortcake (e.g. strawberry) but use ¼ cup sugar instead of 4 teaspoons to make a sweeter dough.

Scottish Shortbread
Jeanie Thomson Simpson
Thanks to Virginia Crisler Simpson

1 cup butter

¾ cup sugar

1 egg yolk

2 ¼ cups all purpose flour

Cream butter and sugar, add egg yolk. Add flour and stir until blended. Place on bread board and knead until smooth. Bake in greased round cake pan at 325 º for 1 hour. Do not over bake—makes it too dry. Cut apart bite-size wedges while still warm. Allow to cool in pan.

Finnan Haddie
Jeanie Thomson Simpson

1# smoked haddock

1 large onion, thinly sliced

1 ¾ cups milk

½ teaspoon cracked black pepper

1 ½ teaspoons mustard powder

1 tablespoon butter, softened

2 teaspoons all-purpose flour

1 finely chopped (spring) green onion
Finely chopped parsley (for garnish)

Place the thinly sliced onion in the base of a large pan. Cut the smoked haddock into pieces about ½ - 1" wide and spread over onion. Mix the milk, pepper and mustard and pour over the fish. Bring to a boil slowly, reduce the heat to low and simmer covered for about 5 minutes. Then uncover and simmer for another five minutes. Remove the fish from the pan with a slotted spoon to allow the juices to run off and place in a warm serving dish. Continue to simmer the mixture in the pan for another five minutes, stirring frequently. Mix the warm butter and flour and add to the pan along with the finely chopped spring onion. Stir over a low heat until the mixture comes to a slow boil and thickens slightly. Pour over the fish and serve with some finely chopped parsley for garnish.

Mince and Tatties
Jeanie Thomson Simpson

1 tablespoon oil
1 large onion, finely chopped
1 # ground beef
2 medium carrots, sliced
1 tablespoon toasted pinhead oatmeal
Water to cover
1 to 2 beef stock cubes
Salt and pepper to taste
3 teaspoons corn starch

Heat the oil in a pan and sauté the onion until it is dark brown. Add in the ground beef and cook until well browned. Add the carrots and oatmeal, mix well and pour in enough water to just cover. Crumble in the stock cubes, season and stir well. Once the mince is cooked, thicken mice with about 3 teaspoons of corn starch mixed with a little cold water. Serve mince with boiled potatoes.

Oatmeal Stuffing
Jeanie Thomson Simpson
Adapted by Leslie Simpson Hall

½ cup finely minced celery
2 tablespoons finely minced onion
2 tablespoons butter or margarine
¾ cup Quaker Old-Fashioned Oats
Salt and pepper to taste
Sufficient boiling water to moisten oats mixture

Sauté celery and onion in melted butter or margarine until vegetables are tender. Add dry oats, salt and pepper and enough boiling water to barely moisten mixture. Don't make too wet! Use to stuff a hen prior to roasting.

Corn Relish
Jennie Crisler

18 large ears corn
3 red peppers
3 green peppers
8 onions
4 large cucumbers
1 or 2 small heads of cabbage chopped
¼ cup mustard seed
5 cups brown sugar
½ cup salt
1 tablespoon turmeric powder
2 bunches of celery

Mix all and cover with vinegar and cook for 45 minutes. Then process in water bath in canning jars. (Note: Jennie wrote "if vinegar is real strong, dilute with 1/3 to ½ parts water."

Chili Sauce
Jennie Crisler

24 ripe tomatoes
8 large onions
6 green peppers
5 cups apple cider vinegar
Salt to taste
1 teaspoon cinnamon
½ teaspoon ground cloves
1 teaspoon black pepper

Peel tomatoes. Dice and chop onions and peppers. Mix all together and boil until vegetables are tender and thickened, three hours or longer. (Jennie wrote "I weaken the vinegar half and half when the tomatoes are small. I sorta' estimate the amount.")

Mashed Potato Fondant
Jennie Crisler

½ cup mashed potatoes
2 teaspoons soft butter
Dash of salt
½ cup finely chopped nuts (if desired)
1 teaspoon vanilla extract
1 ½ teaspoon almond extract
4 ½ cup confectioner's sugar

Mix mashed potatoes with butter, a few grains of salt, nuts (if used), and flavorings. Then work in sugar, kneading until it makes a smooth fondant. Shape as desired. Can be used to fill whole dates at Christmas and add to a cookie tray.

Chicken Casserole
Jennie Crisler
Thanks to Doris Jean Crisler Campbell

4 whole chicken breast, split and boned
1 box Uncle Ben's Wild Rice (long grain with seasoning)
1 can chow mien vegetables
1 can sliced water chestnuts
1 can cream of mushroom soup
1 can cream of celery soup
1 soup can of water
1 medium onion, chopped

Place rice with seasonings in bottom of 9 x 13" baking pan. Place uncooked chicken on top of rice. Mix together remaining ingredients and pour over chicken. Bake one hour at 350 degrees.

Oil Sugar Cookies
Jennie Crisler
Thanks to Doris Jean Crisler Campbell

1 cup oleo-margarine
1 cup white sugar
1 cup confectioner's sugar
2 eggs
2 teaspoons vanilla extract
4 cups all-purpose flour
1 teaspoon baking soda
1 teaspoon cream of tartar
½ teaspoon salt
1 cup cooking oil (I use Crisco)

Cream together first three ingredients. Add eggs and vanilla extract. Mix in dry ingredients alternately with cooking oil. Mixture will be very soft. Put in refrigerator for several hours, or better still overnight. Make in small balls. Place on cookie sheet and press with fork. Bake at 350 degrees for about 12 minutes. Makes 10-12 dozen.

Warehouse Blue Cheese Dressing
Jennie Crisler
Thanks to Doris Jean Crisler Campbell

4 ounces crumbled blue cheese
1 cup mayonnaise
¼ cup salad oil
¼ cup sour cream
¼ cup buttermilk
1 tablespoon vinegar
½ teaspoon salt
Dash of garlic powder

Mix all ingredients together. Keep refrigerated.

Suet Pudding
Minnie Hopkins Crisler
Thanks to Doris Jean Crisler Campbell

1 cup chopped suet
1 cup raisins
1 cup sugar
1 cup sour milk
1 teaspoon baking soda in milk
Cinnamon and nutmeg to taste
Pinch of salt
Mix all ingredients to make thick as for cake. Steam for 3 hours. Serve with lemon sauce.

Lemon Sauce
Jennie Crisler
Thanks to Virginia Crisler Simpson

Mix 1 cup brown sugar with 1 tablespoon flour in sauce pan. Add 1 cup boiling water. Cook until thickened. Add about 1 teaspoon lemon juice and 3-4 slices of thinly sliced lemon. Serve warm over plum pudding or suet pudding.

Descendants of James Simpson

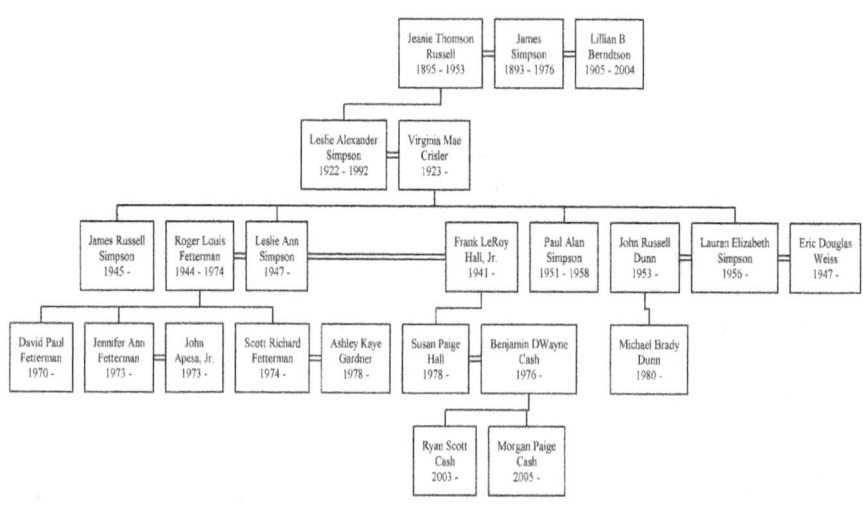

Descendants of Orval Hamilton Crisler

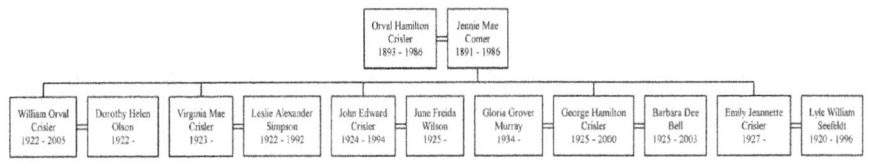

147

Endnotes

1 Katherine Scott Sturdevant, *Bringing Your Family History to Life through Social History* (Cincinnati, Ohio: Betterway Books, 2000), 6.

2 Orval Hamilton Crisler, birth certificate, Newton County Health Department, Morocco, IN.

3 Most Popular 1000 Names of the 1890's, Social Security Online, http://www.ssa.gov/OACT/babynames/decades/names1890s.html, downloaded 3 June 2008.

4 William Neville Crisler, Jr., *A Genealogy, History and Chronology of The Kreisler—Crisler Family of the United States of America or More Particularly the Descendants of Matthais Kreisler and Barbara Von Schellenberg Kreisler* (Waco, Texas: Texian Press, 1981), 3-5.

5 Hamilton Crisler entry, *A History of Warren, Benton, Jasper and Newton Counties Indiana,* CD-ROM (Chicago, Illinois: F. A. Battey and Company, 1883), 798.

6 Family data, Hamilton Crisler Family Bible, original in 2008 in the hands of Charles Timothy Crisler, PO Box 12913, Norwood, OH, 45212. The Hamilton Crisler Family Bible passed from Hamilton to his son William Addison, to his son Orval Hamilton, to Orval's eldest son, William Orval, and to Peter William Crisler.

7 Hamilton Crisler household, 1880 U.S. Census, Newton County, Indiana, population schedule, township of Jackson, page 2, supervisor's district 5, enumeration district #130, dwelling #13, family #13, Family History film 1254301; Page 234.2000, Image 0466.

8 Newton County Indiana, *Index to Marriage Record 1860-1920.* Inclusive Volume, Original Record Located: County Clerk's Office, Book: 20, Page 219.

9 Orval Hamilton Crisler, birth certificate, Newton County Health Department, Morocco, IN.

10 Daguerreotype, Wikipedia, online, http://en.wikipedia.org/wiki/Daguerreotype, downloaded 2 June 2008.

11 George Eastman, Wikipedia, online, http://en.wikipedia.org/wiki/George_Eastman, downloaded 2 June, 2008.

12 Jasper-Newton Counties Genealogical Society, *History of Newton County Indiana 1985* (Dallas, Texas: Taylor Publishing Company, 1985), 157.

13 Get Your Grip on History, Living History Farms, online, http://www.lhf.org/cgi-bin/gygsite.pl. downloaded 4 March, 2008.

14 Jasper-Newton Counties Genealogical Society, *History of Newton County Indiana,* 157.

15 Daniel Nelson, *Farm and Factory: Workers in the Midwest 1880-1990* (Bloomington, Indiana: Indiana University Press, 1995), 12.

16 The Gilpin Sulky Plow, John Deere, online, http://www.deere.com/en_US/compinfo/student/gilpinplow.html, downloaded 3 March 2008.

17 Daniel Nelson, *Farm and Factory: Workers in the Midwest 1880-1990,* 19-20.

18 Jeduthan Hopkins household, 1860 U. S. Census, Stark County, Illinois, population schedule, Valley township, Valley, post office, page 153, dwelling # 1035, family # 1006; National Archives micropublication M563, roll 229.

19 Get Your Grip on History, Living History Farms, online, http://www.lhf.org/cgi-bin/gygsite.pl, downloaded 4 March, 2008.

20 Cottage Cheese, Essortment, online, http://www.essortment.com/all/makecottageche_rloh.htm, downloaded 5 March, 2008.

21 Get Your Grip on History, Living History Farms, online, http:www.lfh.org/cgi-bin/gygactivity.pl, downloaded 4 March, 2008.

22 Get Your Grip on History, Living History Farms, online, http://www.lhf.org/cgi-bin/gygsite.pl,. downloaded 4 March, 2008.

23 Jasper-Newton Counties Genealogical Society, *History of Newton County, Indiana,* 156.

[24] Daniel Nelson, *Farm and Factory: Workers in the Midwest 1880-1990*, 19-20.

[25] Historical Boy's Clothing, online, http://histclo.com/chron/c1900.html, downloaded 4 March, 2008.

[26] William Addison Crisler obituary, "The Rensselaer Republican", Rensselaer, Indiana, June 13, 1911.

[27] Pre 1920 News and Interesting Tidbits, The People History, online, http://thepeoplehistory.blogspot.com/2007/09/league-of-nations-1919.html, downloaded 1 June 2008.

[28] William Addison Crisler inventory Claim File #5, Estate # 893, Jasper County Circuit Court, Rensselaer, Indiana.

[29] Jennie Gleason obituary, *Rensselaer Republican*, Rensselaer, Indiana, December 17, 1891.

[30] Newton County, Indiana Marriage Book, County Clerk's Office, Kentland, Indiana.

[31] Jennie Gleason obituary, *Rensselaer Republican*, Rensselaer, Indiana, December 17, 1891.

[32] Puerperal Fever, Britannica Online Encyclopedia, online, http:www.britannica.com/eb/article-9061826/puerperal-fever. downloaded 15 January, 2008.

[33] Mary A. Comer entry, Hendricks County Death Record, Number 934, County Clerk's Office, Danville, Indiana.

[34] William Cyrus Comer, death certificate number 31309, Indiana State Department of Health, Indianapolis, Indiana.

[35] William C. Comer tombstone, Weston Cemetery, Rensselaer (Jasper County), Indiana; transcribed by the author 11 September 2007.

[36] William C. Comer obituary, *Rensselaer Republic, Rensselaer, Indiana, December 31, 1926.*

[37] Mrs. Jennie Comer obituary, *Rensselaer Republican*, Rensselaer, Indiana, December 17, 1891, page 1, column 4.

[38] John E. Comer, Bureau of Land Management Land Patent issued September 10, 1838 at Crawfordsville, Indiana for 80 acres in Indiana, Document # 30187, Accession/Serial # IN3220_.342 BLM Serial # IN NO S/N.

[39] Louis Hamilton., *A Standard History of Jasper and Newton Counties Indiana*, 520-521.

[40] John E. Comer and Mazilla Comer tombstones, Weston Cemetery, Rensselaer (Jasper County), Indiana; transcribed by the author 11 September 2007.

[41] Jesse Comer tombstone, Barkley Cemetery, Jasper County, Indiana; transcribed by the author 11 September 2007.

[42] Oliver Gleason file, no. 310633, Declaration for Pension, dated April 3, 1915.

[43] Oliver Gleason file, no. 310633, Declaration for Pension, dated April 3, 1915.

[44] Oliver Gleason file, no. 310633, Declaration for Pension, dated April 3, 1915.

[45] Oliver Gleason household, 1880 US census, Newton County, Indiana, population schedule, Lincoln township, Family History Library film # 1254301, NA film # TD-0301, Page # 221D.

[46] Thomas Gleason entry, *International Genealogical Index (IGI)* (Salt Lake City: Family History Library, 1999), citing Batch # 8932405, sheet #24, Source Call # 1553625.

[47] Crockery History Group, The *Crockery Collection: A History of Crockery Township* (Nunica, Michigan: Rogers Printing, 1994), Volume 1, 57.

[48] Crockery History Group, *The Crockery Collection: A History of Crockery Township,* Volume II, 24.

[49] Crockery History Group, *The Crockery Collection: A History of Crockery Township,* Volume I, 58.

[50] Crockery History Group, *The Crockery Collection: A History of Crockery Township,* Volume I, 84.

[51] Crockery History Group, *The Crockery Collection: A History of Crockery Township,* Volume I, 37.

[52] Crockery History Group, *The Crockery Collection: A History of Crockery Township,* Volume I, 98.

[53] Mrs. Oliver Gleason, Sr. obituary, *Grand Haven Daily Tribune,* Grand Haven, Michigan, March 10, 1899.

[54] E. S. Mason household, 1900 U. S. census, Ottawa County, Michigan, population schedule, Crockery Township, enumeration district 118, supervisor's district 5, dwelling 251, family 253, National Archives and Records Administration, 1900, roll T623.

55 William D. Middleton, George M. Smerk, and Roberta L. Diehl, editors, *Encyclopedia of North American Railroads,* (Bloomington, Indiana: Indiana University Press, 2007), 559.

56 Lizzie Comer household, 1900 U. S. census, Jasper County, Indiana, population schedule, city of Rensselaer, enumeration district 20, supervisor's district 10, sheet 5A, dwelling 92, family 94; National Archives and Records Administration, 1900. T623.

57 Boarding Houses, Hearth to Hearth Article, Journal of Antiques, online, http://www.journalofantiques.com/Mar03/hearthmar03.htm, downloaded 7 March, 2008.

58 Elizabeth Comer obituary, *Rensselaer Republican*, Rensselaer, Indiana, December 26, 1933.

59 Mary Comer obituary, *Rensselaer Republican*, Rensselaer, Indiana, October 4, 1935.

60 Vincent Tompkins, editor, *American Decade 1900—1909* (Detroit, Michigan: Gale Research, 1996), 175.

61 Vincent Tompkins, editor, *American Decade 1900—1909*, 176.

62 Wesley Memorial Hospital, *Wesley Memorial Hospital School for Nurses Brochure*, Chicago, Ill, 1912-1913.

63 Wesley Memorial Hospital, *Wesley Memorial Hospital School for Nurses Brochure*, Chicago, Ill, 1912-1913.

64 Wesley Memorial Hospital, *Wesley Memorial Hospital School for Nurses Brochure*, Chicago, Ill, 1912-1913.

65 Susan M. Sacharski, *To Be a Nurse*, (Chicago, Illinois: Northwestern Memorial Hospital, 1990), 40.

66 Susan M. Sacharski, *To Be a Nurse*, 29.

67 Article on Antique Engagement Rings, About.com, online, http://weddings.about.com/od/weddingorengagementrings/a/AntiqueRings.htm, downloaded 20 May 2008.

68 Application for Marriage License, Jasper County, Indiana, dated September 30, 1920.

69 French Lick Indiana, Wikipedia, online, http://en.wikipedia.org/wiki/French_Lick,_Indiana, downloaded 20 November 2007.

70 Harvey Green, *The Uncertainty of Everyday Life, 1915—1945*, (New York, Harper Collins, 1992), 62.

[71] Leslie C. McDaniel, "Getting a Charge out of Delcos: Collector Restores 'Power of the Post', www.farmcollector.com, downloaded 9 January 2008.

[72] Telephone, Wikipedia, online, http://en.wikipedia.org/wiki/Telephone, downloaded 12 January 2008.

[73] Telephone History, Telephone Museum, online, http://www.telephonymuseum.com/History%201901-1940.htm, downloaded 19 November 2007.

[74] Pyloric Stenosis, Medicine Net, online, http://www.medicinenet.com/pernicious_anemia/article.htm, downloaded 12 November 2007.

[75] Pyloric Stenosis, Kids Health, online, www.kidshealth.org, downloaded 11 November 2007.

[76] Wesley Hospital School for Nurses Brochure, Chicago, 1912-1913.

[77] Stephen Mintz and Susan Kellogg, *Domestic Revolutions: A Social History of American Family Life*, (New York: Free Press, 1988), 109-110.

[78] David E. Kyvig, *Daily Life in the United States, 1920—1930: Decades of Promise and Pain*, (Westport, Connecticut: Greenwood Press, 2002), 7.

[79] Brief History of Birth Control, Our Bodies Ourselves, online, http://www.ourbodiesourselves.org/book/companion.asp?id=18&compID=53, downloaded 3 December 2007.

[80] Daniel Nelson, *Farm and Factory: Workers in the Midwest 1880—1990*, 15.

[81] Benjamin Franklin Bailey, "*Present Status of Pediatrics*", State Journal Company, 1896, 305.

[82] Kyvig, *Daily Life in the United States*, 10.

[83] Kyvig, *Daily Life in the United States*, 11.

[84] LaSalle Extension University, Wikipedia, online, http://en.wikipedia.org/wiki/La_Salle_Extension_University, downloaded 13 December 2007.

[85] E-mail from Thomas Bockman, Secretary of Glen Ellyn Lodge #95 dated 2 March 2008.

[86] Waukegan, Illinois, Wikipedia, online, http://en.wikipedia.org/wiki/Waukegan,_Illinois, downloaded 15 May 2008.

[87] Outboard Marine Corporation, Funding Universe, online, http://www.fundinguniverse.com/company-histories/Outboard-Marine-Corporation-Company-History.html, downloaded 15 May 2008.

[88] At Home, 20's Style, Lisa's Nostalgia Café, online, http://en.wikipedia.org/wiki/La_Salle_Extension_University, downloaded 26 March 2008.

[89] Harvey Green, *The Uncertainty of Everyday Life, 1915—1945*, 110.

[90] At Home, 20's Style, Lisa's Nostalgia Café , online, http://en.wikipedia.org/wiki/La_Salle_Extension_University, downloaded 26 March 2008.

[91] At Home, 20's Style, Lisa's Nostalgia Café, online, http://en.wikipedia.org/wiki/La_Salle_Extension_University, downloaded 26 March 2008.

[92] Razor, Wikipedia online, http://en.wikipedia.org/wiki/Razor, downloaded 15 May 2008.

[93] General Electric, online, http://www.otal.umd.edu/~vg/amst205.F97/vj11/project5.html, downloaded 10 September, 2008.

[94] Hoosier Cabinet, Wikipedia, online, http://en.wikipedia.org/wiki/Hoosier_cabinet, downloaded 27 March 2008.

[95] 1920's Food, 1920—1930, online, http://www.1920-30.com/food, downloaded 27 March 2008.

[96] Bluing (Fabric), Wikipedia, online, http://en.wikipedia.org/wiki/Laundry_bluing, downloaded 4 April 2008.

[97] Kyvig, *Daily Life in the United States,* 125.

[98] Orval H. Crisler household, 1930 U. S. Census, Lake County, Illinois, population schedule, city of Waukegan, enumeration district [ED] 49-78, supervisor's district [SD] 3, sheet 42B, dwelling 617, family 1022, National Archives and Records Administration 1930 T 626, roll 530.

[99] Marc McCutcheon, *The Writer's Guide to Everyday Life from Prohibition through World War I,* (Cincinnati, OH: Writer's Digest Books, 1995), 181.

[100] Great Depression, Encyclopedia of Chicago online, www.encyclopedia.chicagohistory.org, downloaded March, 2008.

[101] Chicago during the Great Depression, Roosevelt University, Chicago (Schaumburg) online, www.roosevelt.edu/chicagohistory, downloaded 7 March, 2008.

[102] Kyvig, *Daily Life in the United States,* 191.

[103] Chicago World's Fair: A Century of Progress Exposition 1933—1934, AOL Hometown, online, http://hometown.aol.com/chicfair/, downloaded 10 March 2008.

[104] Social Security (United States), Wikipedia online, http://en.wikipedia.org/wiki/Social_Security_(United_States), downloaded 4 April 2008.

[105] Ronald H. Bailey, *The Home Front: USA,* (Alexandria, Virginia, Time Life Books: 1977), 110.

[106] Gasoline Rationing on the Home Front in WW II, Pre-War Buick website online. http://www.prewarbuick.com/features/your_car_is_a_war_now, downloaded 4 April 2008.

[107] Ronald H. Bailey, *The Home Front: USA*, 108.

[108] Victory Gardens, Wikipedia online, http://en.wikipedia.org/wiki/Victory_garden, downloaded 4 April 2008.

[109] Women in War Jobs—Rosie the Riveter 1942—1945, Ad Council online, www.adcouncil.org, downloaded 4 April 2008.

[110] Post-World War II Baby Boom, Wikipedia, online, http://en.wikipedia.org/wiki/Post-World_War_II_baby_boom, downloaded 6 April 2008.

[111] The Evolution of Childbirth, Suite 101, online, http://www.suite101.com/article.cfm/pregnancy_empowerment/58918, downloaded 15 March 2008.

[112] The History of Childbirth—Ouch!, The History of Net, online, http://www.thehistoryof.net/history-of-childbirth.html, downloaded 7 December 2007.

[113] Glen Ellyn Illinois, online http://www.glen-ellyn.com, downloaded 30 March 2008.

[114] R. Conrad Stein, *Scotland, (New York: Children's Press, 2001)*, 61.

[115] The Second City of the Empire—The 19th Century, Welcome to Glasgow, online, http://www.glasgow.gov.uk/en/AboutGlasgow/History/The+Second+City.htm, downloaded 22 June 2008

[116] History, Clydebank Restoration Trust, online, http://www.clydebankrestoration.com/history, downloaded 19 June 2008.

[117] Scotland's Maritime Legacy, Scotland online, http://www.scotland.org/aboutinnovations-and-creativity/features/education/maritime.html, downloaded 20 June 2008.

[118] The Second City of the Empire—1830s to 1914, The Glasgow Story, online, http://www.theglasgowstory.com/storyd.php, downloaded 26 November 2007.

[119] Fred M. Walker, *Song of the Clyde: A History of Clyde Shipbuilding*, (New York: W. W. Norton & Company, 1984), 4.

[120] Patricia Levy, *Cultures of the World—Scotland*, (New York: Marshall Cavendish, 2000), 15.

[121] Gordon Menzies, editor, *In Search of Scotland*, (Lanham, Maryland: Roberts Rinehart Publishers, 2001),194.

[122] Patricia Levy, *Cultures of the World—Scotland*, 96.

[123]Tenement House, The National Trust for Scotland, online, http://www. nts.org.uk/Property/59/Details/, downloaded 22 June 2008.

[124] Helen Clark and Elizabeth Carnegie, *She Was Aye Workin'* (Oxford, England: White Cockade Publishing, 2003), 15.

[125] Apartment Building, Wikipedia, online, http://en.wikipedia.org/wiki/ Apartment_building, downloaded 22 June 2008.

[126] Jean Faley, *Up Oor Close* (Wendlebury, Oxon: White Cockade Publishing, 1990), 40.

[127] Linoleum, Wikipedia, online, http://en.wikipedia.org/wiki/Linoleum, downloaded 23 July 2008.

[128] Jeannie Thomas at her range in a typical tenement kitchen, 1920's, Glasgow Digital Library online, http://gdl.cdlr.strath.ac.uk/springburn/ spring027.htm, downloaded 23 July 2008.

[129] Clotted Cream, Wikipedia, online, http://en.wikipedia.org/wiki/Clotted_ cream, downloaded 2 September 2008.

[130] Scone (bread), Wikipedia, online, http://en.wikipedia.org/wiki/Scone_ (bread), downloaded 23 July 2008.

[131] A Brief History of Marzipan and Marzipan Confections, online, http:// www.marzipanconfections.com/history.html, downloaded 27 July 2008.

[132] Clark and Carnegie, *She Was Aye Workin'*, 106.

[133] Faley, *Up Oor Close* , 49.

[134] Clark and Carnegie, *She Was Aye Workin'*, 108.

[135] Faley, *Up Oor Close* , 52.

[136] Faley, *Up Oor Close* , 55.

[137] Faley, *Up Oor Close* ,105.

[138] Laundry Blue, Old and Interesting, online, http://www.oldandinteresting. com/laundry-blue.aspx, downloaded 27 July, 2008.

[139] Clark and Carnegie, *She Was Aye Workin'*, 115.

[140] Scots Mark New Year With Fiery Ancient Rites, National Geographic News ,online, December 31, 2002, http://news.nationalgeographic.com/ news/2002/12/1230_021231_hogmanay.html, downloaded 26 July 2008.

[141] General Themes—Transport, The Clydebank Story, online, http://www. theclydebankstory.com, downloaded 20 June 2008.

[142] Kinning Park, Wikipedia, online, http://en.wikipedia.org/wiki/Kinning_Park, downloaded 29 July 2008.

[143] Clark and Carnegie, 84.

[144] Clark and Carnegie, 79.

[145] Edward Jenner, Wikipedia, online, http://en.wikipedia.org/wiki/Edward_Jenner, downloaded 1 August 2008.

[146] Smallpox Disease Overview, Centers for Disease Control, online, http://www.bt.cdc.gov/agent/smallpox/overview/disease-facts.asp, downloaded 1 August 2008.

[147] Education and Training in Scotland National Dossier 2004, Scottish Government Publications, online, http://www.scotland.gov.uk/Publications/2004/06/19476/38581, downloaded 1 August 2008.

[148] No Mean City: 1914 to 1950s, The Glasgow Story, online, http://www.theglasgowstory.com/story, downloaded 26 November 2007.

[149] Tawse, Wikipedia, online, http://en.wikipedia.org/wiki/Tawse, downloaded 1 August 2008.

[150] T. C. Smout, *A Century of The Scottish People*, (London: Fontana Press, 1986), 103.

[151] Shipbuilders, Ancestral Scotland, online, http://www.ancestralscotland.com/research-your-roots/working-men-and-women/909585/, downloaded 2 August 2008.

[152] Faley, *Up Oor Close,* 20.

[153] Jeanie Thomson Russell, birth certificate no. 451,Extract Entry of Birth, District of Govan in the County of Lanark, Glasgow.

[154] Crofting in Scotland, Tour Scotland, online, http://www.fife.50megs.com/crofts.htm, downloaded 13 August 2008.

[155] Introduction—The Govan Story, online, http://www.thegovanstory.co.uk/introduction.php, downloaded 9 August 2008.

[156] Govan, Wikipedia, online, http://en.wikipedia.org/wiki/Govan, downloaded 9 August 2008.

[157] T. C. Smout, *A Century of the Scottish People, 1830—1950,* 85.

[158] Scottish Wedding Announcements, Past and Present, Loch Lomond Net, online, http://www.loch-lomond.net/weddings/index.asp, downloaded 13 August 2008.

[159] Did You Know? Marriage Customs in Scotland, Rampant Scotland, online, http://www.rampantscotland.com/know/blknow/marriage.htm, downloaded 13 August 2008.

[160] Scotland's Music, online, http://www.scotlandsmusic.com/scottish-wedding-traditions.htm, downloaded 13 August 2008.

[161] Leslie Alexander Simpson, birth certificate, no. 1381 Extract Entry of Birth District of Govan in the County of Lanark, Glasgow, Scotland.

[162] On This Day in Scottish History, BBC, online, http://www.bbc.co.uk/scotland/history/onthisday/may/6, downloaded 19 August 2008.

[163] Linthouse, Wikipedia online, http://en.wikipedia.org/wiki/Linthouse, downloaded 27 August 2008.

[164] T. C. Smout, *A Century of the Scottish People 1830—1950,* 114.

[165] James Meek, *The Land and People of Scotland,* (New York: Harper Collins, 1990), 182.

[166] The Scots Empire, online, http:www.channel4.com/learning, downloaded 5 August 2008.

[167] Emigration, online, http:www.scan.org.uk/knowledgebase/topics/emigration topic, downloaded 5 August 2008.

[168] Immigration Act of 1924, online, http:www.wikipedia.org/wiki/Immigration Act of 1924, downloaded 5 August 2008.

[169] John F. Kennedy, *A Nation of Immigrants* (New York: Harper & Row, 1964), 4.

[170] Motoring, Encyclopedia of Chicago, online, http://www.encyclopedia.chicagohistory.org/pages/846.html, downloaded 21 August 2008.

[171] Crane Company, The Electronic History of Chicago, online, http://www.encyclopedia.chicagohistory.org/pages/2633.html downloaded 16 August 2008.

[172] Crossing Borders: Scottish emigration to Canada, History in Focus, online, http://www.history.ac.uk/ihr/Focus/Migration/articles/harper.html, downloaded 26 November 2007.

[173] Great Depression, Chicago History, online, http://www.encyclopedia.chicagohistory.org/pages/542.html, downloaded 25 August 2008.

[174] Clark and Carnegie, *She Was Aye Workin',* 77.

[175] Pennsylvania Railroad, Wikipedia, online, http://en.wikipedia.org/wiki/Pennsylvania Railroad, downloaded 3 September 2008.

[176] The War Years—1940s, Quartermaster, online, http://www.quarterdeck. org/book/1940s.htm, downloaded 1 September 2008.

[177] Clydebank Blitz, online, http://en.wikipedia.org/wiki/Glasgow_Blitz, downloaded 3 September 2008.

[178]American Cultural History, 1950—1959, Lone Star College-Kingwood online, http://kclibrary.lonestar.edu/decade50.html, downloaded 11 September 2008.

[179] Admiral Television Set 1954, Flickr online, http://flickr.com/photos/ 16841984@N05/2524341525/, downloaded 21 September 2008.

[180]Douglas DC-6, online, http://flickr.com/photos/ 16841984@N05/2524341525/, downloaded 21 September, 2008.

www.ingramcontent.com/pod-product-compliance
Lightning Source LLC
Chambersburg PA
CBHW060624290526
45793CB00001B/128